Scot Free

Elizabeth Bell

Copyright © 2013 Elizabeth Bell

ISBN-13:978-0-615-82474-1

Photos contributed by Elizabeth Bell

Although inspired by actual events and people some names have been changed to protect the privacy of those mentioned in the memoirs and some of the book may be fictional.

FORWARD

In the mid seventies I got a call from Scottie who was trying to gather together a dozen or so old friends for a "looking back" and "looking inward" weekend at her home in Rockland. That was the start of an annual event which has been a treasure for all of us. We go now to Scottie's cottage on Howard Pond and we bring yearbooks, photo albums, rubber rafts, food, memories and an often bizarre sense of humor. The time together used to be filled with hilarity and practical jokes--a break from the child rearing years. However life has a way of making us more reflective, more sober. Two of the group have lost adult children--one to the war in Iraq and one to cancer. The normal wear and tear of life has made us appreciate the support of this group and we do still laugh---a lot.

Linwood, Cassandra, Scottie, Peter

We grew up in a time when people did not talk about the painful things that were going on at home. We were taught that family problems were generally left in the family. Scottie suffered particularly from this secrecy and it breaks my heart to think about what she went through dealing with the post traumatic stress and subsequent alcoholism of her father. It also breaks my heart to realize what her mother suffered during those years. Scottie's mother was a wonderful teacher and influenced us all in a very positive way.

Scottie's memoirs tell of these often difficult childhood years through her own troubled marriage and subsequent health issues. She also tells of her innovative successes with her job which provided satisfaction, travel and adventure. And always, through good times and bad, she raised her children with strength and sensitivity.

SCOT FREE

With the support of her second husband Jim and her own creativity Scottie has told her story. The story takes us all up some very high mountains and into some deep valleys. It is a priceless gift to Rhonda and Robbie and the rest of her friends and family. It is a priceless gift to all of us who have loved her for almost seven decades.

Cassandra Cousins Wright

DEDICATION

This memoir, Scot Free, is dedicated to all the children too afraid to tell.

THANK YOU

Thank you Robert Stowell, Rhonda Stowell, Jim Bell, Dennis Davis, Cassandra Wright, Carole Spruce, BonnyFreeman, Donna Yates, Elizabeth Aarts, Jane Flahive, Isabel Bitting, Nancy Olmsted, Betty Cooper and Cela Vellines for advice and encouragement.

We did it!

AUTHOR'S INTRODUCTION

A year ago, my son Rob told me he thought I should write my memoirs. My daughter Rhonda agreed and offered to edit. I was flattered because I am not a good writer but Rob is. I haven't written two consecutive pages of anything since I was in school but I think now that they may have felt it would be fun for me. They were right. Although the order of years and place may be confusing and I certainly don't have an extensive vocabulary or didn't set up the story paying attention to style or composition, I have written my story. It was enjoyable to reminisce and as I thought of one memory it led to another. I found myself just floating along with pen in hand.

This is my account of growing up in Maine in the 50s and 60s and is entirely from my perspective. It has brought mixed feelings of joy and heart break as I have put my past in print. Some of those days were wonderful, some were not so wonderful, but many were drastically different from the way we live today.

Scottie Bell

TABLE OF CONTENTS

1. Orono * Old Town the early years 1

2. Old Town * Pets remain in our hearts forever 21

3. Rockland * a special place 26

4. Fear * life changers 39

5. Growing Up * music to our ears 44

6. Bethel * Hanover 60

7. War Seeps through Generations * families left destroyed 68

8. Moving On * marriage and a new generation 71

9. Social Change * total confusion 83

10. HPWATS * my BFFs 90

11. Deep Sorrow * my life crashes 97

12. God Within Us 102

13. Lost Feelings * broken vows 106

14. Bye Barb, Bye Dad * loss of unconditional love 111

15. Fulfillment * making a difference 120

16. Jim, King Bubba 134

ONE

ORONO * ORONO
The early years, ages 1-12
1944 - 1956

My very first memory was looking up from my crib and seeing a man with a mustache and in uniform looking down at me. I liked it when he came as Mom and Dad seemed to enjoy him and laughed a lot when he was visiting. The small room had an orange glow as an electrical cord and one light bulb dangled down from the ceiling. Years later I learned that he was Benny Webster of Bangor and he and Dad both served in World War 11 and went to the University of Maine together. Ben became a CPA in Bangor. Dad took me to visit Ben when I was an adult and worked in Bangor and even then he had us laughing although he was very ill. He joked,
   "I won't be buying any green bananas."

Maine photo courtesy of Peter Devine.

He passed away shortly after our visit and Dad and I were grateful we had that time with him. Sometimes childhood experiences never surface again and never become memories to be relived. I discovered that as I thought of one experience, another came to mind. I can still recall struggling to reach up and touch the door knob when I was living in Orono. I was three or four when Dad lifted me up over his head so I could balance on his one hand and touch the kitchen ceiling. We would dance with my feet on his shoes and he taught me the words to "The Maine Stein Song" as we walked hand in hand on Forest Avenue in Orono. Dad was a tall man and had black curly hair. I felt very secure with him and loved being with him. Sometimes we listened to the Paul Whitman Show on the radio and Dad would ask me to name the instruments as they were played. I learned most of them and loved those special times with my father.

When I was four, brother Jim was two and he tragically rolled from a cot up against a radiator and burned the back of his head. I can still hear his screams as Mom rushed in and called an ambulance. Mom said the worst thing she ever had to do was wipe his hair off that radiator. Throughout his life Jim had a large scar on the back of his head. He would either wear a toupee or grow the back of his hair long to cover it up.

Shortly after that I watched from the upstairs window in the Orono house as Bumpa, my Dad's father arrived in his new Buick and drove up the driveway. Mom and Grammie Blanche got out with Grammie carrying our baby sister Barbara Jean home from the hospital. She was born on Memorial Day and the weather was sunny and warm. The window was open and a breeze blew the sheer curtains. Jim was in his crib in back of me jumping up and down and giggling.

Soon after Barbara joined us, we moved to an upstairs apartment located between the Herbert Gray Elementary School and the high school in Old Town. Stillwater Avenue was a beautiful wide street with elms shading it on both sides. Everyone knew everyone on the street then and the neighbors were very friendly. Doors were never locked and people would visit homes without calling first. When we first moved to Old Town we had a flag pole on the side lawn and my mother used to put a blanket on the grass and we would picnic there. Mom had long reddish hair and I thought she was beautiful. She was. She was a caring, loving person and I loved her so much. She taught us songs like the 'Teddy Bears' Picnic,' 'Always', the 'Sunny Side of the Street,' and 'Tea For Two,' and other popular songs.

We had an ice box in our apartment and the ice man would climb the wooden stairs added to the outside of the house and carry large blocks of ice into the house with tongs. Then he would put the ice into the bottom of the ice box in our kitchen. Milk was delivered to the house too. Mom would order three glass quart bottles at a time three times weekly and would give us a spoonful of cream from the top of the milk before she set the rest aside for baking. Mom cooked and baked every day. Most mothers I knew did. Few women worked. While living upstairs we didn't have a bath tub and would bathe in a galvanized tub placed on the kitchen floor. We three kids all bathed together on Saturday nights.

Scottie, Jim and Barbie enjoying a bath. Small pieces of soap were saved and put in the bubble maker Scottie is holding. The tin dishes held by Jim and Barbie were Jello molds.

Spring, fall, and winter were spent in Old Town and summer was spent at camp in Hanover. In Old Town I watched as Stillwater Avenue was paved.

I was sitting on the front porch with Mama and we saw a girl walking down the other side of the street with her hand held by her mother as they headed to the small corner store, Berry's Store. Mama spoke to them and they crossed the street to visit us. Both mothers wore colorful spring dresses. The girl's name was Donna and I pictured her name printed over and over on my door when I went to bed that night. I wanted to remember Donna because I thought she would be a good friend. Donna was five, I was four.

Donna lived across the street from my family and I spent much of my time with Donna and her folks as I grew up. We would drive to their camp on Beech Hill Pond in Otis, rain or shine. Hurricane weather was the best time to go for her Dad loved the excitement of it and wanted to check on their camp. When the weather was good, we would spend the entire day in the water there and we both became experts at holding our breath, looking at each other and singing under water. I loved Donna's parents and they were like a Mom and Dad to me. At their camp as I got older, I slept in the top bunk and one night a huge wood spider came out on the wall near my head. Mr. Fayle sprayed with an insecticide and other big spiders came out from everywhere, or so it seemed. I jumped off that bunk into his arms as fast as I could. I couldn't get off that bed fast enough. Everyone laughed but I didn't think it was funny at all.

Brother Jim, Barbie and I missed Mom when she went to the Old Town Hospital but it was all worth it when she came home with a new brother, Robert Alan. I was six when Bobby was born and at Donna's house across the street when they arrived home. Donna and I ran over as Mom carried the baby upstairs. He was wrapped in a blue blanket and we were allowed to hold my brother. He was little and it was an exciting event for my family. Now Mom and Dad had four children. In our household I was the oldest child and Dad would refer to us kids as brats. It was to him an endearing expression and I didn't mind it. I felt he was proud to have us and we strived to please him.

There was a circular porch to the left of our house and two big bushes in the front where we would play. We kids would bring out Mom's three afghans and hang them from the branches making forts or hammocks with them. We always found ways to keep busy and went out to our hammocks after meeting Bobby. Sometimes we would spend the entire day outside playing games with others in the neighborhood. Some favorites were "Kick the Can," "Simon Says," and "Red Rover," but if it rained and we stayed inside my

Mom would tell stories such as the one about walking on jello, making it a special day. Mom was a very good storyteller, very demonstrative and creative, and we loved her cackling voice and antics as she played one of the three witches in Macbeth.

There was also a neighborhood gathering place nearby, a frog pond which iced over in the winter where we would ice skate and slide. Dad would take me there and pull me around on a sled as he skated and because he was fast, a speed skater, I felt like I was flying.

Barb, Jim, Scottie and Bob at a lake we were visiting.

We also liked going to see the popcorn man when he was in town because he had a monkey on a leash that sat on top of a popcorn machine. The man would crank a large lever and music would play as the monkey danced around. The popcorn was good, too. Sometimes Donna and I would scootch and slide under the fence behind my house to the high school track and play in a cluster of pines there. It was like another world, peaceful and beautiful. We children knew our neighborhoods well.

Occasionally we had babysitters we weren't fond of and we didn't always behave well and would give some of them a hard time. We would not go to bed when we were told, but we had one sitter named Pat and we were good with her. We liked her. One morning the kerosene stove in the kitchen flared up and the flame almost hit the ceiling. We kids were standing in the doorway ready to run out but Pat got it under control. I had Bobby in my arms and Jimmy and Barbie right by my sides and I held my breath because I knew that Dad had lost his house to fire when he was twelve and in our upstairs apartment a friend of Dads caught a book of matches on fire and burned his hand. I saw it happen. My brother and father were both burned on the back of their heads. Dad was burned in the war and Jim on a radiator and both had toupees. I always have been scared to death of fire.

One summer night our parents left us home while they played cards next door. We didn't have a sitter and were told to go to bed at nine but stayed up and around midnight called in to a radio station we were listening to and asked if they would play "Davy Crockett" and dedicate it to Jim, Barbie, Bobby and Scottie. Before the song ended my parents were home. The radio had been on at our neighbors, too. They weren't upset and we were tremendously relieved. Music was always a big part of my family's life. Dad played the banjo, drums, mandolin, and harmonica. Jim played the tuba and bass viol and piano. Bobby played the drums and I tried to play the clarinet, piano and snare drum and the whole family harmonized. Barbie and I would even perform for some of the local fraternal clubs singing, "It's Only a Shanty in Old Shanty Town." Mom tried to persuade me to sing alto but I didn't because I thought it was too manly. She never knew.

Once in a while we were allowed to walk up to the store at the corner of Fourth Street and Stillwater Avenue. The proprietors carried a great selection of penny candy, much more than Berry's store. When I was going into the store one day an elderly man gave me a penny that he had just picked up from ice on the ground. I knew who he was and had seen his wife so I accepted it so I could buy an extra piece of candy. He was always kind to kids and that got around. I thanked him more than once and thought it was most generous of him.

In the early fifties, Dad came home from Boston with a television set. We could only get snow on the screen and eventually a test pattern and the first black and white show, "Boston Blackie," a detective show out of Boston. We could hardly see the picture but people from all over the area came into the living room to see a television. We later got a piece of plastic with blue on top, yellow in the middle and green on the bottom which would stick to the screen simulating color. 'Pinky Lee,' 'Howdy Doody,' and the 'Big Top,' were our favorites but we liked the Westerns too. There were realistic shows and Western stars, the "Lone Ranger," Gene Autry, Dale Evans, Roy Rogers and Tonto. My entire class was invited over after school and we watched the snowy images on television. Mama made popcorn and we set up chairs in front of the television. Soon NBC entered the Bangor market and television became popular.

As a normal procedure in elementary schools, policemen came into my classroom in Old Town to fingerprint all the students. We were told a day ahead of time that they were coming. I remember wondering if I should go to school or pretend to be sick the next day and stay home. What if I became a bad person when I grew up? I didn't want anyone to have my fingerprints. They did take my prints. I was nine, a fourth grader.

For two years I would have nightmares that I would remember in the morning and they would swirl around in my mind all day. The dream was the same each time. I was in the woods running as fast as I could on my hands and knees. A huge bull dog was chasing me and kept pinching me with its paw. The dream was frightening. After many nights having this dream over a two year period, I suddenly figured out that the bull dog represented my father and his paw, Dad's thumb. His thumb had been reconstructed with skin after he was burned in the war. Once I figured that out, I never had that dream again. I was around nine when the dreams started. Was I becoming afraid of my father?

I would try very hard to get to sleep right after going to bed because I would dread it when Dad got home late at night. He would throw up and was loud doing it. It just sent shivers through me and it happened often. There was little relief from the sadness I felt. Sometimes I would crawl under the bed with my pillow and try to cover my ears. One day I climbed up on the toilet seat in the small bathroom and with a steak knife I scratched in bold letters into the black woodwork way up high, "I hate my Dad when he is dr...."

I never finished it and it was up high enough so no one knew it was there. Years later after the house was sold, Barbie took me through the house to see the new renovations because a friend of hers lived there then and had invited Barb in to see the changes. I joined her and peeked into the bathroom and my scratching was still in the black woodwork up near the bathroom ceiling. Still no one knew it was there and I still had a tremendous amount of anger thinking back to the time I wrote it.

In the sixth grade I took ballroom dancing lessons and wore the same dress Nana had sent me, to dance class every week. My mother would pin a fake red rose on the waist area to make it look different. I wondered if I really was poor but didn't know if I was or not. The other girls had more than one dress.

We kids decided to have a surprise anniversary party for our parents. I made invitations and years later learned from Mom that the pencil drawn invitations had a pile of presents sketched on the front of them. We hoped their friends would bring gifts. I don't know if the invites were mailed or hand delivered but the idea worked. That night people started coming in the door, presents in hand, filling the living room. Dad borrowed alcohol from neighbors and although we had snacks out in fancy dishes, Mom got more food out. The party was a huge success and Mom told me later that people from different groups attended, she introduced guests to each other, and they had a great time. We kids were so proud of ourselves and I was amazed at how easy it had been to bring people together.

Those were carefree days. Our parents never worried about us and if they wanted us to come home from playing outside they would simply yell our names from their front doors. Often another neighbor outside would chime in. We respected our elders and never called them by their first names. It was always Mr. Curtis or Mrs. Martin.

There were eight or ten kids who played together in our neighborhood throughout our school years. Neighbors Sue and Donna were born on the same day, Valentine's Day, and their parents would alternate hosting a large birthday party for them. I looked forward to their special day as it gave all of us a chance to dress up and get together. I still remember my unhappiness when I couldn't attend Kenny's birthday party because I had the chicken pox. Mrs. Moors delivered some cake and favors to our house and I felt much better but the feelings of being left out of something bothered me.

The children on our street would write and produce outdoor summer shows for their parents to attend. One of the most memorable was a wedding between Donna and Ken long before they were teens. The chairs were all lined up in Sue's driveway and bows were tied to the aisle chairs where the 'bride' and 'groom' walked down the aisle to stand before the child judge. The costumes were very original, too. I did tap dance one time but most summers we were away at camp when the shows were presented and I couldn't participate.

Donna and I would sometimes sit on her side lawn which was somewhat secluded, and eat Saltine crackers from between our toes. We were both limber of course, had to be to accomplish such a feat. Mr. Fayle thought Donna was mature enough to have her own charge account at Berry's store. We were both delighted and trotted to the store and bought fudgesicles. We parked ourselves on Donna's side lawn and ate them. It was a hot day and they tasted so good we returned to the store and bought another, and went back for another and another. We purchased one at a time. After six or seven trips to the store and back, her Dad found out what we were doing, probably from the store owner, and he yelled at us both, particularly at Donna. He told her she wasn't as mature as he thought she was. I had never heard him holler like that. That was the end of Donna's charge account. Donna and I remain best friends to this day. She's mature now.

Dancing has always been my first love. I began tap dancing at four years old and can picture myself doing step shuffle ball change, the waltz clog, around the large room at the church on the hill in Bangor. Later the Thomas School of Dance moved to its own building, a large Victorian on Broadway. The first year that Polly Thomas created her own dance line, the Thomasettes, I was selected and thrilled. Some of her former students danced with the Rockettes at Radio City Music Hall in New York and returned to teach at the dancing school. I wasn't good enough and didn't have the drive or desire to move away from home and felt I was headed to college so never took dancing seriously. As a child I was Topsy in "Uncle Tom's Cabin" and toured with the Maine State Ballet Company.

I remember sitting in the back seat of a car with strangers as we returned home from a performance. I was about ten and felt very adult. Every year we had a dance recital and I would stay awake the night before worrying about it. The productions were creative and costumes lavish. I think the biggest reward for me was eating in a restaurant afterwards because that was an annual occurrence and I was allowed to stay out late. Sometimes Dad would drive me the thirteen miles to dancing school and on the way home would stop at Narah's store in Old Town and buy me a coke. That was a huge gift to me then, but most often I rode to dancing school on a public bus. Through all of this I felt lucky in a number of ways including the opportunities my parents gave me in ballet, tap and pointe lessons in Bangor.

As we were growing up we always had to be at the dinner table at six o'clock no matter where we were or what we were doing. Mom would have a balanced meal on the table and we were expected to clean our plates. Mom liked to cook and we knew when she put her apron on she was about to cook supper. Tripe and tongue and heart were some of my favorites but I haven't eaten them since. I would stand in the kitchen and watch as Dad gutted birds or fish on newspapers on the linoleum floor. I also saw him do the same thing to a deer out in the big barn out back of the house and thought it was all perfectly fine. I liked venison too, but Barb hated it all. She one day sat at the table all afternoon missing school because she wouldn't eat her venison. I still picture her with tears in her eyes as I had to leave her and head back to afternoon classes. I wanted to cry too.

We brats found a solution to take care of the food we disliked. It was a great idea. We soon learned to cough venison or anything we didn't like into a napkin and place it up on a shelf we located under the large dining room table. Only we knew. A few years later we cleaned out the shelf and it was loaded with crumpled napkins and food harder than bricks.

Our dining room table was a good place for conversation and arguments. Our meals were always lively and Mom would often let us invite our friends for supper and they would call their parents to get permission to stay. Children were respectful to their parents then and didn't question the house rules.

In most households the evening meal was held with the entire family at the table and often breakfast was eaten together too, creating opportunities for additional family bonding. It was much different than the way it is today. School hours were from eight to three with an hour at noontime for lunch. We learned how to protect ourselves from a bomb by hiding under our desks and had practice much like students have fire drills today.

During the Korean War when I was very young I volunteered to help at a tower on Jefferson Street, I believe, where we watched for planes flying over Old Town. I could see them coming but couldn't identify them but thought the duty was very important.

If Donna and I weren't together, we were on the phone....for hours. Our phone was in the living room and the cord was long enough so I could go into the closet to talk. Sometimes it would be hours before Mom missed me and told me to get off the phone. My parents just couldn't understand how two people could be together all day and still have something to say to each other on the phone at night.

The holidays were exciting and since my parents didn't buy a lot for us during the year, we were inundated with gifts. I would do a Christmas countdown beginning the first of December and loved the gift opening. I also have memories of the year I was more excited to see the gift I gave to someone else opened than their present to me. I was probably twenty-five. No, only kidding. As a family we would go into the woods to cut down a fresh tree for decorating. I didn't always enjoy it because it was cold and the snow could be knee deep, getting down into our boots, but it was a special day when we were all together. Decorating the house was fun but putting the tree up was very stressful. My Dad just didn't have the patience it took to get the tree up and straight in good spirits. That was a time I wanted to be out of the house.

On Christmas Eve Jim and I would stay awake until it was almost time to go downstairs and open our stockings. Wow, we were excited. I felt I was the luckiest girl on earth. I was given a wind up monkey that played cymbals and a little printing press one year which were a couple of my favorites. Mom always picked out gifts that seemed to be made exclusively for us.

At Christmas time Donna and I couldn't wait to see each others presents and would visit after we had opened the gifts under our trees. One Christmas Eve Donna swore she heard Rudolph on her porch roof. I had just stopped believing in Santa then and hoped so much she was right but I just didn't believe it was really Rudolph. Maybe her brother Dickie played a trick on her and she suggested that maybe Dickie had put the reindeer prints in the snow she saw on the roof. The next Christmas brought many changes and we didn't believe in Santa. There were changes in the next year.

Our entire family became stressed particularly on holidays, and its carefree and happy spirit was changing because Dad was drinking way too much. Christmas was still a special day and Mom made sure it was filled with the smell of turkey and homemade pies, but I could feel the tension. Early on Christmas Day we kids would go downstairs for our stockings which eventually became a long nylon stocking and then had to wait for Dad to get out of bed to have breakfast and open presents. It took hours and was often noon before he got up and it was excruciating. Mom would more than make up for it and give us a happy holiday. She would join us kids in love and would sing but I still missed our Dad and I felt he had begun to change.

When Mom worked teaching part time she was home most of the time. She read a lot but she was very unhappy. She was an exceptional mother and it was hard for me to see her crying as often as I did.

Dad was out of control. He had a girlfriend, Carol, and he even brought her to our house with another couple. They played bridge and Mom waited on them. It made me sick. Mom should not have confided as much as she did with me at age thirteen, but she didn't have anyone else to talk to. I hated Carol and blamed her for Mom's unhappiness. I even sent her a letter telling her how we felt and Barb and Jim signed it with me. Bob was too young. Mom told me that our letter did no good. Carol still stayed with Dad. A situation like that is so misunderstood and exaggerated in the mind of a young person. It hurt so much. I didn't think of anything else and had no idea why Dad would hurt Mom so much. I ached for her. I even dreamt of taking Dad's gun, and hiding in the back seat of his car and killing Carol. I thought how I didn't want to go to prison but at least I would have time to do my art work there, uninterrupted. Later on Dad had another girl friend, Joan and I met her at camp. I knew she was his girlfriend because they were acting silly and she called him Cookie. Wow, that hurt. I hated her too and I hated Dad.

The change of seasons played a major role in my life. To me it was a meaningful process and each new season had an affect on me as well as on this good earth. Spring in Maine smelled fresh like grass, and a light green color symbolized the earth's new life. Each year as the lawns were mowed for the first time the air smelled new and brought an inner excitement. Summer was outdoor fun time. I always referred to it as my favorite season because we could swim. I looked forward to summer vacation because I could play outside with my friends all day as long as I was home at six for supper. Fall was spectacular. Piling the leaves up into a heap and jumping into them sent out a crunch sound only heard by doing that.

The burning leaves had a unique smell that clearly meant that fall had arrived. The colorful trees warmed my heart. Maine is absolutely gorgeous, and fall brought with it the knowledge that holidays were coming soon. When I was involved in playing winter sports I didn't want to see the season end. Sliding on a toboggan at the Pig Farm in Stillwater with a group of friends, skiing, skating and building snowmen shortened the winter season. When the fresh snow sparkled it seemed like a new beginning.

In winter, Donna and I built snow forts together in the snow piled up by the plows next to the road side. One of the best forts had small shelves carved out in the walls where we put candles. It was so neat. We also became real pros at making forts from lx2x60" sticks of wood stored by the Old Town Canoe Company as woodpiles near our homes. Some of our wood forts were quite high with adjoining rooms. There were also fort fights and some bad boys would tear down our architecturally perfect forts. We still know who they are. I kept telling myself, we are all God's children as Mom had instilled in me but they scared me.

I took the bus to swim classes at Gilman Falls Avenue and to the municipal pool in Orono, where I was taught to dive. On my very first attempt, I dove off the side of the pool and went straight down into the water hitting my head on the bottom of the pool. I couldn't swim back up. Two lifeguards came in after me and although I was hurting I refused an ambulance and sat by the side of the pool a long time before going home by myself, by bus. I was back at the Orono pool to swim the next day. I had won a race with the breast stroke at that pool and loved competitive swimming. I thought then that I would like to work to become a better swimmer and compete. For several summers when I was older, I attended the Girl Scout Camp at Cold Stream Pond in

Lincoln and eventually I became a camp counselor there. I had a dynamic swimming instructor and became a certified "swimmer" through the Red Cross.

A week or two each summer I was away from home at summer camp and I missed my parents although I loved meeting new girls and boys and doing the outdoor activities and the crafts. One trip to a children's camp was by train from Bangor to Winthrop. Donna and I went together to camp a couple of times. I think it was three times. I went to Camp Tanglewood or the Methodist Church Camp for one or two weeks in the summer. Mom wrote nearly every day and she and Dad would visit on Parents' Weekend. For one visit Mom wore her navy dress with white polka dots and her white pearls. I loved that dress. Dad wore a sport coat and they looked wonderful and happy. In one letter Mom mentioned that they had a surprise waiting for me when I got home and I thought of everything, there were so many different kinds of surprises. On arriving home it was difficult to act grateful with a rooster and hen on the back porch but I think I did it. It was a surprise!

Our family went on picnics and tented and fished in Northern Maine, often on weekends. On one trip, when we were joined by the Curtis family, we headed up Route two with two cars, two canoes and all the gear. The weather was warm and the area around the pond smelled like pine needles. We launched both canoes which were overloaded with people and gear and we headed to a deserted island that we could see from shore. Our canoe capsized and other than Dad losing a camera and our lunch we had no problems and we all managed to get to shore. I was very frightened but held onto the canoe until Dad could get each one of us to the island. We kids spent much of the day exploring the island, picking blueberries, and wishing we had dry clothes. Since Dad worked outdoors, he taught me to be comfortable in the woods even by myself. I always felt confident in the forest and enjoyed the crunch of pine needles underfoot, the spruce, fir, and pine trees, and the light filtering through the tree boughs as it hit the ground. He would teach me the names of trees, plants, and birds and showed me how to survive on spring water, fresh fiddleheads and berries. I knew not to pick a Lady Slipper or Jack in the Pulpit, endangered plants in Maine at the time.

Sometimes he would stop the car and say he had to see a moose and he would then walk into the woods for a few minutes. Since I had seen him dissect a moose with other biologists and wardens I believed he was seeing a moose. When I told Mama I wanted to go see the moose too she laughed because when Dad made a brief stop to see one, he was going to the bathroom. I was embarrassed.

Dad took me out in his canoe when he counted woodcock by listening to their call or to a road block while he counted deer. For a week during summers we would head north to Frost Pond. Our family would travel in a station wagon named the "Bluebird" or sit in the back of a panel truck with no windows which was an invitation for car sickness. The travel was awful but we had a great time once we reached our destination. Sometimes we tented, other times we stayed in wardens' camps which were often the only camp on the pond.

I remember catching a seventeen inch pickerel at Sandy Pond and noticing Dad's proud expression. It was fun to fish, and at Frost Pond I walked right up to a huge moose when I was on a trail heading towards the spring for water. The moose was probably fifteen or twenty feet ahead of me on the path. I had a pail with me and simply turned and walked back to the camp.

At Frost Pond Camps we kids would spend time catching bloodsuckers. If one of them should die while we were playing with them we buried them and placed a cross made of sticks over them. We would even say a little prayer. One time we put several blood suckers in a large coffee can and placed it on the porch railing with a board and a rock on top. In the morning the bloodsuckers had all disappeared and the can was just how we left it. No one admitted letting them go and I am still stumped about that one. How did they get out?

We also had watermelon seed spitting contests at Frost Pond Camps. We would eat watermelon and spit the seeds as far as we could across the porch to see who could hit the furthest crack between the floor boards as the seed would disappear under. The more seeds that hit their mark the better, but we sure ate plenty of watermelon to play the game. I don't remember who won but I do know that to this day I don't like watermelon. Who knows? There could be tons of watermelons growing under that porch.

Pete the Fox

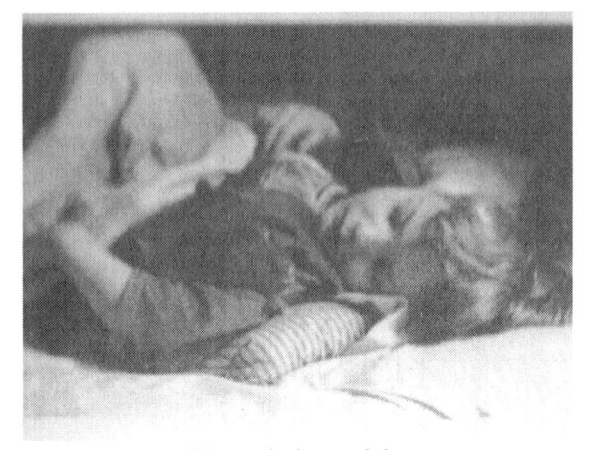

Jimmy and Suzie the bear cub having a nap.

A brook flows through the forest. Screw Auger Falls

TWO

OLD TOWN
Pets Remain In Our Hearts
1944-1956

Dad loved animals and as part of his work he would bring wounded or abandoned animals into our house to nurse them back to good health so they could be released to the wild. My favorite pet was Sparkie the deer. One leg had been amputated by an industrial grass cutter and reattached by Doc Whitter at the University of Maine in Orono. She was a fawn and played with Princess and Wampum, our English setters. Dad occasionally would set the three animals free in the back yard and they would race back and forth. Our neighbors would come out to watch them too. The three animals got along well together. Unfortunately the reattachment failed but with three legs Sparkie could at times out run the dogs. The fawn would sleep in bed with us and we had her for almost a year. The day we took her to the game farm in Gray to release her was difficult although she was in a beautifully wooded, enclosed, safe place. When we drove the car into the farm area, her eyes opened wide and her ears perked up when she heard the other deer. She immediately communicated with them. It was a wonderful place to leave her and heartwarming to see her joy. We all cried but we were happy for her.

Another of my favorite pets, Pete the fox, was special too. He was so well trained that we could walk him on a leash. The kit was thin and we worked to fatten him up. He visited with us at Howard Pond and spent the summer with us at a camp on Hadley Lake in Machias where Dad was working temporarily. We could let Pete out at the camp and he would return when called for supper. One night when Dad returned from work, Pete the fox was waiting at the door. He then ran behind the refrigerator and kept peering out at Dad. Finally as Dad got into his sleeping bag, he felt something unusual at his feet. Pete had left him a dead frog. When Dad retrieved it, the fox came out into the room and jumped up and down. He was thrilled with his gift for my Dad. When one night Pete didn't return home for supper, Dad found out that a farmer down the road had shot him as he was threatening his chickens. We were devastated. Other animals we had in our house in Old Town included bears in the barn, a beaver in the bathtub, Snoopy and Spooky, baby raccoons in the cellar, and a mink among many others. Mom was not happy when she went downstairs into the cellar to get some jars of mincemeat and discovered that the raccoons had opened some of the covers and eaten some of the venison based pie filling. An attorney in town told me that he never forgot his surprise when he visited us when he was a child and a duck came out from behind the Christmas tree. I did well in my science classes because Dad would bring an animal to school with a story to share with the students.

One of the abandoned animals we had freely roamed around the kitchen. A porcupine. Dad had taught me how to scooch down and let the animal walk up one arm, go across my shoulders, and kind of waddle down the other arm. She had a sweet disposition and I was aware that if I touched her back I could get quills but her belly was smooth and had none. She would play with the small kittens we had and one day the porcupine and one of the kittens began rolling around playing and ended up under the black stove.

Bobby feeding the porcupine.

Bobby and Barbie feeding Sparkie the fawn.

I immediately reached under to rescue the cat who honestly didn't need rescuing, but instead I picked up the porcupine. It took Dad a while to get the quills out of my hand as they have prongs which open up under the skin making it a painful ordeal. My whole family watched as he took each quill out with tweezers.

Another time we had a wolf in our den. He was the only animal that frightened me. Dad could go in there and even pat it but we kids had to keep away from it. Other Fish and Wildlife employees would stop in to look at it because that particular animal was a rarity in our part of the country. Many animals had to be nursed with milk in baby bottles and we would carry them around in our arms. They would stay with us for several months. I don't think the wolf was with us more than a week.

While in my mother's classroom at the high school, one of our classmates Kenny looked out the window and said there was a strange animal in the parking lot. We all went to the window and I recognized Woody, our woodchuck. He had somehow wandered away from his cage and escaped from our shed. When the bell rang signaling the class change, several of my classmates joined me outside and we circled Woody and captured him in someone's coat. I took him home and that afternoon Dad gave me permission to take him out into the woods and release him to the wild. It was gratifying to see him back in his environment, healthy at last.

There has been research done now showing the benefits of pet ownership to the elderly. Having access to a pet and patting a pet can lower the heart rate and improve health. I have always wanted to rescue every needy animal I have seen and the caring has filtered down through generations. Pets have always been very important members of our family. Brother Bob, Rob, Rhonda, Jackie, Sean, Shay, Cheryl, Mike and Geoff all have pets. Pets are family. They listen, comfort, and give kisses. I have always felt thankful to my mother who let a home become so much more when she agreed to have so many animals running around.

THREE

ROCKLAND
A special place
1956-1960

My younger sister Barbie and I spent part of our summers in Rockland in the fifties and sixties. My grandmother and great grandparents had a large, welcoming home with mahogany woodwork and furniture and oriental rugs throughout. The old pantry next to the kitchen had shelves on three walls with large crock pots, jars of pickles, and canned goods lined nearly to the ceiling. It didn't take long for us to find the doughnut crock. When we were little, Sis and I would take our freshly made doughnuts through the back shed outside and eat them while sitting on a stone wall. It was our special place and we had glass and tin tea sets and would play by the wall with our small metal toy stove and make mud pies for our dolls. The Rockland household had a cook who came in regularly and baked in the black stove in the kitchen. I don't remember her name because Barb and I didn't spend much time there for it always seemed we were in the way. There were usually a few kittens running around in the kitchen, too. There was also a live-in housekeeper, Helen, and I remember her for her sense of humor. She was standoffish and quiet at first but eventually felt comfortable speaking to us. She acted up and would make faces at us when no one was looking to make us laugh. A petite woman with brown hair pulled back, she wore a white uniform and apron. She made sure that Barbie and I had everything we needed.

My great grandmother, Grammie Bird, was gray haired, petite and very formal. I was conscious of my posture just walking by her. She didn't criticize us but I never knew how she felt about me. Years later I met a woman who had worked at the market down the street in the forties and fifties and delivered groceries to the Bird residence. She still remembered with disdain having to enter the shed only through the back door to deliver groceries to the Bird family.

My great grandfather, Adonirum Judson Bird, was outgoing, tall, and loved to play with us. When we were young, he would hide pennies in one of his hands which would be ours if we guessed the correct hand. He also had a spittoon next to his chair although I didn't know what it was then, and often a cat on his shoulder. We called him Papa.

Adonirum Judson Bird, Papa

Great great grandmother wearing the woven hair of her mother in a gold brooch.

A Chinese worker aboard one of Papa's ships wove hair of my great-great great grandmother, and placed it within a beautiful gold brooch.

Grammie, his wife, and my great grandmother would freshen the pillows behind his back and bring him tea. He spent much of his time in his library surrounded by bookshelves, pipes and the odor of pages from old books. He enjoyed telling stories and sister Barbie and I liked to sit on the floor at his knee and listen to them. He told of once taking a shovel to the shore about a half mile from his blueberry barrens and burying several gold coins in the sand. He went home, sketched out a treasure map, dirtied it, and placed it where his best friend could find it. On a sunny day shortly thereafter, the two of them went out to search for treasure. His friend found the coins! Totally unexpected to Papa, photographers from Maine newspapers took pictures of the "find" and interviewed them about their good fortune. It made quite a stir. Papa never "fessed" up.

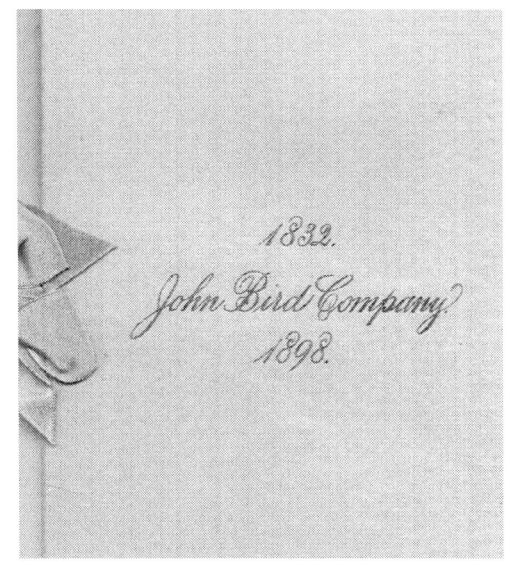

The invitation to the Opening of the Bird block on Tillson Avenue in Rockland.

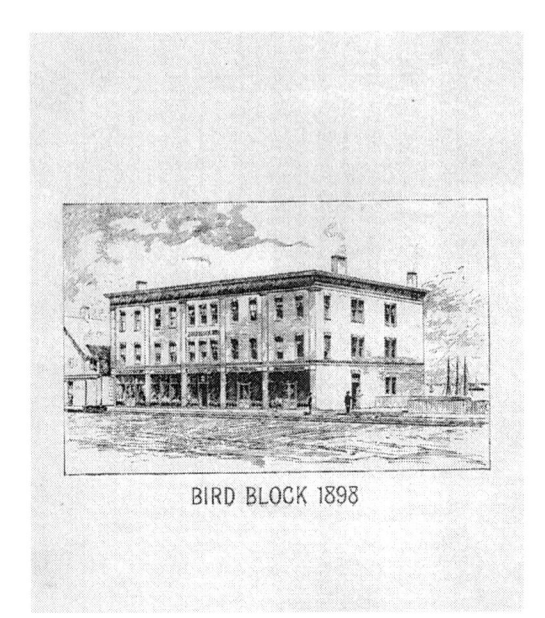

Drawing of the Bird block.

Papa's patent application for the calcium pencil.

Papa was very successful in the shipping trade and transported spices from China to Maine. In the early 1900s Papa was an owner of several businesses and a fleet of ships. He also had an interest in a cement plant, nearly one hundred acres of blueberry fields in St. George, and was active on several business boards. One of his buildings on Tillson Avenue in Rockland has the name Bird carved in cement at the top and it was later owned by the U.S. government and used by the Coast Guard. Papa also invented a calcium pencil but was beaten to the patent office by another industrious inventor.

Nana, his daughter and my grandmother, worked as the assistant city tax assessor, retired and was called back and remained employed into her early seventies. A fun day for Barb and me was a visit to Nana at City Hall. We knew some of the employees there and years later I would meet them again. We had a little desk we sat at and spent our time with coloring books and paper dolls. I designed a paper doll with a purple and pink gown that I thought was absolutely gorgeous. Good grief.

In our early teens, however, Barbie and I became slightly more adventurous. One day we bought some hair color at the five and ten. It was "champagne blonde" and did absolutely nothing to our hair but that night at the family dinner, Barb's forehead started breaking out with red welts. Nana took one look at her and said, "Don't eat any more green beans. You must be allergic to them." She was extremely upset and concerned about Barb and we sisters had all we could do to keep straight faces. When we were much older, we told Nana what we had done. We were laughing when we told her but even then she didn't think it was very funny.

The whistles. I just remembered the whistles and horns tooting. My sister and I as young teens walked down the street to the stores in Rockland in our finest dresses. The more petticoats and the more they were starched, the better. In fact, we would lay them out on the lawn to dry, with as much starch as we could soak into them. When dry, the petticoats would help the dresses with their circular skirts, stand almost straight out around us and we thought we were stylish. We liked the attention too, although we never looked to see who whistled or tooted. We kept walking straight ahead. We would both chuckle.

There was one house we passed on Camden Street with a large side lawn and a hedge all around it. I wondered who lived there and thought about ghosts. We headed to the market with elms shading us as we hugged the sidewalk. At the market, groceries lined the shelves and you could sometimes smell bread but more often than not, the store smelled of fish. The seafood odor always reminded me of Rockland, Maine. Whether traveling to my grandmother's house by car or by Greyhound bus, the fish smell meant we were almost there. The entire city smelled strongly of fish due to the processing plant there.

My grandparents' house had a large dining room with a table that accommodated twelve people and a hutch that covered most of one wall. Crisp white linens were used on the main table with doilies on the smaller ones. On one side of the dining room was a conservatory with windows on one wall, many plants, an orange tree, and a small metal pig we would sit on. The plants were moved occasionally when Grammie Bird hosted the Shakespeare Club and members would rehearse plays wearing detailed costumes with realistic wigs and make-up. A Chamber quartet played in the conservatory. The club originated with Grammie and existed for years. The formal sitting room was at the front of the house and had heavy drapes that touched the floor. It was a darker room and had a fireplace on one wall with a grand piano by another. I don't remember ever seeing anyone in that room and felt lonely when I went in there.

Grammie Bird played the harp which stood between the dining room and conservatory. The front foyer off the sitting room had a huge fancy gold framed mirror on one wall and a large wooden piece of furniture with a storage seat that lifted up in the center, and a high back with a mirror. There were fancy hooks on each side for hanging coats and hats.

Almost everyone who visited wore a hat, had a calling card and was met in the foyer by Helen. The room featured a winding staircase with a light fixture built into the newel post, and a grandfather clock which chimed and produced a loud tic tock. After a night or two I could get to sleep without counting the rhythm.

There was a very large attic over the shed filled with toys. Hundreds of toys. There were dolls, wagons, umbrellas, kimonos, Charleston dresses from the twenties silk hats, mother of pearl opera glasses, and bookcases filled to the brim. By the time we outgrew the attic, everything was gone. I don't know if my grandmother sold the items there or gave them away which was much more likely.

Up the staircase to the second floor was my Aunt Carrie's room. Caroline Jameson was my great grandmother's sister, and her room was filled with books and had pink flowered wallpaper. It seemed that most of the rooms had wallpaper but hers was the most feminine, pink and dainty. The door to her room was always closed and we could never go into her room unless invited. Aunt Carrie moved in with her sister's family as she aged. Her family at one time owned property from Owls Head, Maine, to Jameson Point where the Samoset Resort is located in Rockport. Always single, according to her obituary she was the first woman to graduate from Harvard and was a solo world traveler, unheard of for a woman in those days. I have an album of photographs she took during a trip to Korea.

Aunt Carrie's yard was filled with beautiful wild flowers. She was an avid reader and kept clippings of news articles pertaining to the books, within them. I remember feeling stupid around her and found her difficult to please. Once Barb and I were criticized because we didn't eat the complete apple she gave us. She showed us how we should end up with only the stem, seeds and those tough ear shaped pieces in the center. The core as we knew it didn't exist.

One of the exciting things we experienced with Aunt Carrie was a walk to the Strand Theater in downtown Rockland. We attended the local opening of the movie, "Gone With the Wind" and were dressed up and had our white gloves on as did others there. We sat up straight, didn't talk, and were good throughout the movie and intermission. Aunt Carrie was proud of us. We all loved the movie and talked about it all the way home. When Aunt Carrie eventually moved into the bedroom at Nana's house, we were always quiet when she was there. After she died we didn't have to be quiet upstairs anymore. It was different. More relaxed.

The Camden Street house had a bathroom that was larger than most bedrooms and had two tubs, a regular tub and a small tub for feet washing. We didn't use the little tub much as we got older but when we were very little we used the small tub for bathing especially after making mud pies. It was quite a treat. Barb and I usually slept in the back bedroom upstairs with the starched white curtains and flowery wallpaper. We each had a twin bed and there was a white cupboard in the room with shelves where we kept our things. The ceiling slanted inward on each side of the room and some of the windows were pushed out with a hook holding them open. Although the old Victorian home had heavy draperies downstairs, the bedrooms upstairs had sheer curtains and the rooms were bright and sunny. It is amazing how a home with love can stay with you throughout your lifetime. The Rockland house was that to me.

Nettie Bird Frost, my mother's Mom, was a sweet, kind, and loving woman. Educated at the Katherine Gibbs School in Boston, she was very likeable, somewhat prim and proper, and had a wonderful sense of humor. Her hair was a silvery gray unless she had a new hairdresser and then it would sometimes have a tinge of blue. Appointments with her podiatrist were scheduled regularly. She wore flowered dresses and jewelry even if she were staying home. Nana had a passion for reading and for many years belonged to a romance novel book club and subscribed to a detective tabloid with all its blood and gore.

An avid cook, she would have a large kettle of seafood chowder loaded with lobster ready when Barbie and I visited and loved baking her chewy brownies, cream puffs, and Indian pudding. Later on, when I would grocery shop for her, she would give me a list of things to pick up at the store with their brand names. She loved Stouffer's macaroni and cheese in a box. Any company that advertised on television made a sale to Nana.

Nana lived on Camden Street until her family passed away and she sold her home to a church and sold the farm house and land, too. The house has been torn down. She then moved into a large apartment where she had two cats that kept her company. She groomed them daily and in the fall of each year, Nana would send Barbie and me two new dresses from a fancy children's dress shop on Main Street in Rockland for the start of school. They were the only dresses I had at the time although Mom would sew for us when she could. Nana would occasionally drive from Rockland to Old Town to visit us and arrive with a suitcase and her arms loaded with gifts. She would bring us her old purses filled with combs, candy, pads of paper, etc. I loved those gifts. She would stop at Perry's Nut House in Belfast on the way and pick up cashews in plain white boxes and rock candy. Brothers Bob and Jim would get presents too.

Later on in her life Nana lived in an apartment in our house on Lindsey Street and Rob and Rhonda, my children, visited her daily. Each month one of Nana's women friends would host a bridge party. When it was her month to entertain, I helped my grandmother set up her tables, get the score cards out and put bridge mix candy and cashews out in fancy little dishes. These get togethers lasted many years. Nana lived into her eighties and was dearly loved by many. I think of her often and miss her a lot.

Papa, I was told, had the first car in Rockland. There was a driveway along the conservatory side of the house and I still picture him driving by. The drive became a circle which connected to the street behind the house and there was a barn in back where Papa kept two horses and had a large vegetable garden. He would park his car out back and on weekends the Bird family packed up and headed to the "farm" in St. George. In an isolated coastal area surrounded by blueberry barrens, the 1600 homestead sat alone and nearly untouched since built. Each summer the Bird family would spend a week vacationing there and I milked my first cow at a farm house down the dirt road from there.

My teacher was Dr. Norman Vincent Peale and he began by squirting my face with milk. Barbie couldn't stop laughing. He then gave us some warm milk to drink and we pretended we liked it. Yuck. We thought he was very nice and we could tell that Nana wanted us on our best behavior. She thought he was nice, too.

The homestead had a well-sweep outside with a water pump in the kitchen. Each bedroom had a night stand with a basin and water pitcher for bathing. The beds were piled high with warm quilts and Barbie and I would snuggle together because it could be cold even in the summer. We used kerosene lanterns for light and a huge stone fireplace with a large hanging kettle and built-in ovens on either side was used for heating and cooking. We liked it at the farm and Barb and I didn't find it difficult keeping busy outside during the day. There was a gravel pit nearby with large boulders and we would climb up on them and just talk, watch the butterflies and birds, and gather wildflowers to take back to Nana and Grammie Bird.

When I was eleven I had my first paying job at the farm. I watched the flat bed truck roll across the fields which had been separated and lined with string as the blueberry rakers arrived. Papa taught me how to use a blueberry rake and I found that metal thing extremely heavy. I didn't let on how much my back hurt but pleased Papa by sticking with it if only for half a day. That was enough. Papa tried to convince me to frame my first check but I didn't. I wish I had.

As Barbie and I became young women, Nana saw to it that we were entertained when we were in Rockland. Dance parties were held in the attic and we were introduced to boys and girls whose parents were friends of Nana. Usually there were ten couples, stacks of 45 records and cases of Coke. I would look forward to seeing my Rockland friends in the summer and corresponded with them in the winter, the envy of my junior high school girl friends. Back then Karen, a friend all these years later, brought a letter to school from a boy she had met. Several of us excitedly stood around her as she read it. It wasn't until maybe forty years later that she told us that she had written it herself.

Nana was a divorcee, very rare in those days. She was at one time married to a lawyer, Clark Bradley Frost of Milford, New Hampshire, my grandfather. He was a tall handsome man even though he was somewhat old. Nana told me that the woman my grandfather left her for looked like Bette Davis. We didn't like Bette Davis at all. We knew Grandpa Frost's new wife as Auntie Hill. My mother told me that if I got married and had trouble with my husband and wanted a place to stay for the night, she would not let me into her house. She always felt that Grammie and Papa made it too easy for Nana to return home and move back in with them, and she somewhat blamed them for the divorce. Mom was twelve when her parents divorced. She missed her Dad throughout her lifetime.

Our Mom's father, Grandpa Frost/Clark Bradley Frost.

FOUR

FEAR
Life Changers
1952-1956

I was eight years old. As I had so many times before, I left dancing school and walked down over State Street hill in Bangor to catch a bus and take the one hour trip home to Old Town. It was cold, was getting dark and looked like it was going to snow. There was a man, a big man with a trench coat on and a bottom lip that went over his top one standing at the bus stop. He began asking me questions.

"Where are you getting off?"

When I said, "Elm Street," he said,

"Me, too."

He followed me onto the bus and sat next to me and pushed me in towards the window. He soon began telling me he was going to show me his prick. Thinking it was a needle I began crying and he held out a dime which he said he wanted me to have to stop crying. I kept refusing it. He continued his harassment and the alert bus driver stopped the bus in front of the Maine State Police Barracks in Orono. Two police officers came onto the bus, cuffed the man and took him off the bus. When I arrived home Dad called his friend, the Police Chief in Old Town, who checked on things and told Dad that I would have to testify in court. I was apprehensive and said that I would do it but it was a huge relief to me when a woman sitting behind me on the bus went to court for me. Twelve years later I was working as a secretary at Goldsmith Furniture Company in Old Town and that same man entered the store. I recognized him immediately. I started shaking and after my boss waited on him he told me that the man was from Orono and had recently been released from prison for a child abuse conviction and that he had spent most of this life in jail. I never saw the man again.

When I was around ten, a man in our neighborhood we called Smiley molested me several times. He rode around on a bicycle and would dance the jig for us kids which we all thought was ridiculous. Why did he pick me up? There were other girls and he ignored them. Perhaps I was trying still to please adults and act like a good person. I don't know. I blamed myself and I wasn't to blame. I hated him. A few years ago I discussed this with Donna and she recalled an incident when Smiley had me pinned down under the high bush in front of my house. She said the man was on top of me and that my arms and legs were flailing. I was screaming. She just froze and couldn't get help. I don't recall that particular incident at all. Several months after it all began, I gathered up my courage and told my Mom about his molestation and she told me to stay away from him. I don't know why it took me so long to tell her but the wait was agonizing. Maybe I expected her response and maybe I thought she would blame me. I just didn't know.

In those days unpleasant things were ignored. My mother ignored it. Smiley was killed by a car while riding his bike. I was not unhappy. The damage to a child can show in numerous ways. During the time I was being molested, Mrs Thomas at dancing school was frustrated with me because I wouldn't do a proper plie` (squat). She had one of her instructors choreograph a solo routine for me with plie's throughout the dance. No one ever knew anything was wrong and it wasn't until I came to this point while writing this memoir that I remembered it.

When I was in the sixth grade our family went to Cold Stream Pond to visit our next door neighbors at their camp there. The neighbor was a respected local doctor. While outside, the twenty-nine year old brother of our hostess, the doctor's wife, asked me if I would like to see a fish hatchery. I asked him to repeat the question several times because he had such a strong French accent that I couldn't understand him. Louis pronounced hatchery like hat tree and when I finally understood him, I said sure. I was excited to see a fish hatchery. When we were walking along a wooded path beside the water and looking at the fish, he asked me how much I weighed. I told him I didn't know and he told me he could tell me as he pulled me down on top of him. I struggled to get away from him. I knew his behavior was very wrong when he kissed me, and I finally wriggled free. He gave me his cigarettes and lighter to carry as he swam back to the camp. I was just sick as I walked back into a camp where everyone was congregated and tried to behave as if nothing had happened. It was hard to act normal. I kept the secret from Mom for a week and barely slept. When I finally told her she said,

"You don't have to worry about seeing him. We won't go to that camp again."

Again, ignore it and it will go away. Gail and I watched from her porch across the street from my house as Louis drove by in his blue convertible a couple of times and I was scared to death he would find me but I never saw him again after that week. Somehow I completely set those incidents out of my head and just didn't speak of them. It wasn't until I was in marriage counseling many years later that I described the incidents to my trusted marriage counselor who said,

"I have known women who have spent a lifetime getting over one incident, never three."

She was amazed at what I had been through and that I had kept it to myself. She understood a child's need for approval and support. I later learned that Louis was mentally deranged and had spent many years in prison and in a mental hospital as a sexual offender.

Today child molesters are better understood for the sick creeps they are. They don't get better. Among other things, they physically maim and kill children, ruin a child's life by passing on infectious diseases, causing pregnancies and by making a child lose self-esteem, self confidence and innocence. I became fearful, couldn't sleep, and later found it difficult having successful relationships. I felt guilty about the events and blamed myself for these things happening to me. I had kept everything bottled up inside. I bathed often because I felt so dirty and I didn't want any man to touch me at all. Not even a hand shake. I had been naïve and trusting but my childhood was gone. I didn't trust a soul.

The Stillwater Avenue gang heading to Herbert Gray School for the first day back. The fingers indicate the grades we were attending. Barb was entering kindergarten but copied her big brother, Jim.
Front: Barbie and Jimmy
Back: Sue, her brother Kenny, Cynthia, Donna and Scottie

FIVE

GROWING UP
Music in my life
1952-1962

One day while skating I fell and hit my head. When I was leaving to go home, I took my friend Pam's boots and had an argument with her. I thought they were mine but she explained that mine were new with yellow liners and so I put the new ones on and headed home. Looking down Stillwater Avenue from the top of the hill, my neighborhood looked like a Christmas card. It was covered with snow and like a winter wonderland. The next thing I remember was being in my bed at home and Mom and Dad showing me a doll. I thought that doll was flawless. It seemed like there was a filter in front of my eyes. Dad kept asking me what day it was, and what my name was. I couldn't remember. The doctor came and told us I had suffered a concussion and I spent two weeks out of school. My class wrote get well cards. How I wish I had them today. The time I spent out of school my classmates learned the multiplication tables which I still stumble over today.

My brother Bob had attended the Patriots Football Training Camp when he was in high school. He loved the sport so much. He played football at Old Town High School and after suffering two concussions his doctors would not let him play again. That must have been a very difficult time for him because he was a great player. Concussions are taken very seriously today in both the medical and sports fields and research has increased in that area.

I was in the sixth grade classroom when I heard the name Elvis Presley for the first time. The class bully was teasing a classmate because he had never heard of him. I hadn't either but acted like I had. Backing away slowly as a group began to gather, I did everything to keep the bully's focus off me. When I went home that night I asked Mom who Elvis was and she told me. Mom and Dad didn't like him so I didn't either. A year later I changed my mind as did they. We were all fans and I soon had his 45 records. Liking Elvis was a way for many of us to show a little independence and rebel just a bit. He shook his hips as he sang and many people thought it was horrible, way too sexy for that time. After other singers followed it wasn't an issue anymore. Elvis Presley had just released his first songs and the four of us kids would sing them as we traveled in the car. We knew all the words and I was happy when we sang together.

Jim and Scottie

    Another day I was singing along with Connie Francis on the radio, "Who's Sorry Now," when Mom joined in with all the words. The song had just been rereleased. When she told me the song had been popular in her day I didn't like it as well and was disappointed it wasn't a new song. Mom and I had fun though and learned to play Ricky Nelson's, "I Know Where I'm Going" as a piano duet. At night I would always listen to two radio stations out of Boston and I learned most of the popular rock n roll songs that way. The DJ's were great and I became familiar with the stations and their formats.

    During the winter some of us would go to St. Joseph's skating rink. It was an adventure for me and I would borrow Jane's skates and go regardless of the weather. The best days were those with light snow. There was a little shack on one side of the rink lined with wooden benches inside and it had a black pot belly wood stove in the center. The wood was piled up next to the shack and the heat made the shack very welcoming.

For a couple of days a boy came and sat beside me. We spoke a little and Wayne became my best friend and first love and we were together for three years. He and a friend of his, Doug, practically lived at my house and Wayne became my confidant. My parents liked him and he would pick me up after Girl Scouts and walk me home. I did have some time alone with him but I don't think my parents knew. Sometimes we would skate at the house on the top of Academy Hill. It was absolutely beautiful there as their rink was lighted and lit up the snow.

Some of us kids from the neighborhood would get together and walk to the movies. Goldsmith's Men's Store on Main Street had two revolving doors and we would go into one and out the other each time we walked by. Eventually we were told not to do that again and we didn't dare.

The movie cost twelve cents. When we became a little older the price went up to twenty-five cents and we would see shows like "Oklahoma" or "Summer Place." I clearly remember my skittishness as Cassandra and I walked up Middle Street going home after seeing "Vertigo." Every shadow jumped me and I caught myself holding my breath and eager to get home. It was never a concern then that two young girls were walking home in the dark. It was safe. On our way to the movie a few friends sometimes stopped at Shorette's Restaurant for fried clams, fries and a coke.

Our entire family enjoyed music and when Dad had musicians in the house for jam sessions, Jim and I would quietly move from our bedrooms upstairs, slide down three stairs in our pajamas on our bellies, and lie there and listen to Dixieland. They couldn't see us but we could peek at them. When Jim got older he would put on the album, "Provocative Percussion," and play the bass viol until his fingers bled. He basically taught himself how to play and by the time he was sixteen he belonged to the Musicians' Union and had played in the Bangor and Portland Symphony Orchestras. He was determined to play well and eventually became a recognized jazz bassist throughout the country. It became his profession and his love.

The passage from sixth grade to seventh was very difficult for me. I had felt I was top in the classes until I reached junior high and I was so confused and stressed with my home life it was difficult just keeping up. I practiced writing in a straight line because Donna told me I wouldn't get into junior high school if I didn't. I never could master it but I tried. In one of our classes we had to write a paper about ourselves and our families that was going into our permanent record and I couldn't be truthful. I didn't want to discuss my father's alcoholism with anyone. I did try to write but I erased the paper so much I tore a hole in it. I passed it in without anything written on the page and luckily no one ever discussed it with me.

During my eighth grade year, Dad lost his job along with his biologist partner Joe, due to downsizing. I knew very little about it, particularly about the financial toll it would take on our family. I never knew the reason he was fired. Dad spent a year out of work doing crossword puzzles and entering contests. He sued and was reinstated with back pay and during that time my Mom went to work as a substitute teacher. Dad drank heavily as he had for many years but it had gone beyond weekend binges. Our family was in turmoil.

One day my mother came home and was very excited because a friend's daughter had a box of clothes for me. I was happy too and wore a plaid dress from the box the next day at school. I was proud to have a new dress on when an older girl came up to me and said loudly in front of others,

" I thought that was me walking down the hall when I saw you in my dress." Until that time I never thought about clothes and those unkind words cut through me to the core. That hurt. I still wore the clothes. I avoided the girl.

Scottie wearing clothes from the box given to her.

I don't know why I wondered if I were poor, but I did. The other girls had more than one or two dresses. As a group of us were walking home from school, one of the boys accidently stepped on the back of my shoe.

I had folded my Brownie socks under the heel to hide the holes but I couldn't hide the cardboard in the bottom of the shoe. I was embarrassed even though the boy did say,

"Excuse me."

I can't ever remember asking my parents for clothes. I didn't ever feel I needed good, new clothes or a bureau full of them but I didn't like wearing an old girdle when I ran short on undies. The girdle had also been in the box and I had it on when I unexpectedly went to the doctor after being bitten in my thigh by a German Shepherd. The doctor told me I should not wear something like that and I never mentioned it to anyone. Guess those mothers who told their children to make sure they had on clean underwear in case they had an accident had a point! Popular name brands in clothing were unheard of in those days and keeping up with the Jones' was never an issue.

I have always felt that those who go without material things know throughout their lives that they can survive on very little and make it on their own. There is nowhere to go but up. I had only a few years with very little and it was a minor issue to me then. It didn't bother me much. I borrowed clothes from Gail, Sue and other friends and did well with what I had. Friends are important.

The family, six of us, drove to Milford, N.H. to see my mother's Dad, Grandpa Frost. It was the first time I stayed in a motel. On our drive with two English Setters, a deer and a caged bird in the car, Dad thought he would be humorous and he picked up a hitchhiking sailor. The stranger squeezed into the back seat and afterwards Mom said that she had never seen anyone so eager to get out of a car. Our family was chaotic and loud. Dad was a strong supporter of the military throughout his life and I am sure he wanted to help an active duty sailor but he enjoyed Mom's reaction to his picking up a hitch hiker that day even more.

Mom held Grandpa Frost up on a pedestal. The trip to New Hampshire was my first trip out-of-state and my first visit to Fenway Park to see the Red Sox play baseball. They won 6-5 over the Yankees. Our visit with Grandpa and Auntie Hill was our last. Although he always wrote me, "Dear Betty Scott," a name which was used briefly after my birth, I didn't know Grandpa Frost well. He came to Old Town only once that I recall and we kids slept in the same bed that night. We giggled and just couldn't quiet down.

Mom and Grandpa were talking in the kitchen downstairs when she hollered up the stairs to us,

"Quiet down. I don't want to hear another peep out of you."

Being in our jolly mood we continued with the "peep..peeps" and shook the bed we were laughing so hard. Mom came upstairs and spanked our bottoms with a hairbrush. We were prepared. We had placed encyclopedias down our pajama pants ahead of time. After the spankings we settled down. I didn't know until years later that Mom knew the books were there. If Dad had been home we never would have acted up like that.

In Junior High School some of us bought and wore the same blue jackets and sailor hats we had covered with autographs from our classmates. I think we were thirteen. We looked good but quickly ditched the clothes when a seventh grade rumor spread that we were all pregnant. I thought that was absolutely disgusting. I was twelve when I learned from friends how to get pregnant and I remember looking at my teachers wondering how they could ever do such a thing. I was way behind others my age when it came to the birds and the bees.

On many Sundays, particularly if it rained, my friends and I would set up a few card tables and play cards all day in our living room. Monopoly, Canasta, and Hearts were popular. Sometimes other parents hosted the group for parties. I liked going to Cassandra's house and loved her parents. Her Mom would have home baked sweets for us and even served a meal of steak, peas, and potatoes to us in the front room. Cassandra was with Hoddy and I with Wayne and we had some great times together. During one party there I remember a game we played where we lined up in a row blindfolded and one person would go down the line and kiss each person. Then those in line who had been kissed had to guess who kissed them. I think I remember this game because when I was kissed I guessed it was Wayne and it was Cassandra's mother. How humiliating.

An active social life was important to me and I always thought I had to have a boyfriend because I felt insecure and lonely without one, but I remained a "good girl" until I married. A "good girl"? Now if that term wasn't ridiculous.

There was a group of us that would get together at my house throughout junior and senior high school. They loved my mother as she would always listen to their problems, never judge them, and advise them when they asked. I had several parties in Old Town with twenty or thirty kids and we would play games or dance and play <u>Spin the Bottle.</u> Whoever won or lost, depending on how you looked at it, that couple would go into the closet off the living room to kiss. Many didn't know it, but one side of the closet had a curtain rather than a door, which led directly into the den. My younger sister would sit there in the dark and watch everyone in the closet. Barb was always my little sister and in my view at the time, she spent her days trying to cause trouble between my parents and me. We were typical sisters. We fought like we were enemies when we were young but we always loved each other.

In Junior High School my girlfriends and I were extremely conscious of how we looked. We spent money on Dippity Do hair gel to get the spit curl on our forehead just right. We also wore a string of pop-it beads, and small fake flowers around our hair buns in the back of our heads. Mom told me my hair looked good pulled back, and although severe I could wear it like that. I would baby sit and spend the money I made on new bobby sox for the YMCA Saturday night dances. The socks were only good for a few weeks when the elastic would begin to stretch and they would begin to slip down. Those socks would have to be perfect with our white bucks.

SCOT FREE

The YMCA dances were somewhere to go and have fun every Saturday night and I looked forward to them all week. I went there with the goal of dancing every dance and often I did that with the luxurious smell of Evening in Paris toilet water floating off my body. Loved it. As a sophomore Wayne and I broke up. It broke my heart. He graduated that year and went into the Navy. Just before Wayne returned home from the service he wrote and asked me to wait for him. In those days that meant that your relationship would continue. I agreed. I met up with him briefly when he returned and invited him to camp as I had just driven from camp up to Old Town for that day only. He said he would come but he didn't show up at camp. I was told he went to a dance in Old Town that night. A few weeks later he asked me out and I was in the midst of breaking up with a man I had met during that summer when Wayne was away. Jon was from Duluth, Minnesota, and I liked him but he was way too serious. He was in the Navy stationed in Brunswick and when his mother asked me over the phone what type of wedding I wanted, I knew it had to end. Very cruelly I set up dates with both Wayne and Jon one night. Donna and I watched from her mother's ceramic studio window from across the street. When I got home my mother was furious. Really angry.

"How could you do such a thing? That was a mean thing to do."

She had been the one to answer the door and I think they both came at the same time. I don't know why I did it. I didn't regret it but I later got a card from Wayne with the words,

"I would have sent you a medal but the dime store was closed."

I didn't see Wayne for another thirty years. We were at a high school graduation and he came up to me in the lobby. I was speechless, we said very little, and he couldn't take his eyes off my teenage daughter, Rhonda. I spoke to Jon on the phone a couple of times afterward but never saw him again. After Wayne, I felt I had to be prepared to break up with boyfriends before they broke up with me. It was still very hard and I did feel bad about it but I didn't want to get hurt again. My break up with Wayne hurt, my break up with other boyfriends didn't.

My friend Jane's mother meant the world to me. Dad was very drunk and we were fighting one night when he came after me. I ran straight out the front door and kept on running. It was late and snow was piled up on the ground but I ran not really knowing where I was going. It was absolutely freezing and I didn't have a coat on but I barely noticed I was running so fast. I ran to Jane's and banged on her door all out of breath. Jane's mother was frantic and immediately pulled me into her house. I looked down and I was barefoot. She welcomed me and at my begging, did not call my father. About an hour later Dad came and knocked on her door and Mrs. Wareing gave him a piece of her mind. She really let him have it. He left without me that night. I didn't know if Mrs. Wareing knew about my dysfunctional family before that night but certainly knew she did after that night. I was thankful and relieved she let me stay there and by the time I went home the next day, nothing was said about it.

On birthdays I had wished on nearly every birthday cake as I blew out the candles, that I would be popular. I don't know why I wasted my wishes so, or why that was important to me but my Dad was popular, my grandfather Bumpa was popular and I loved it when they seemed to know everyone they passed on the street. I thought they were special people and everyone seemed to like them. Maybe I still dreamed of pleasing them. I was more than concerned about friends, particularly boys, even though I didn't want them to touch me.

A gift for my sixteenth birthday was a fifth of Barcardi Rum from a friend of Dad's, a State Trooper. What a great role model. I think I had one drink from the bottle. I have no idea what happened to the rest. When Dad drank he was cruel and sloppy. Each day when I woke up I had to decide how I should behave based on his actions. Was he sober or not? I couldn't be myself. It just wasn't fair. I was constantly on guard, on a roller coaster, and was on edge and stressed for years. Later on in marriage counseling I learned two things that would have been helpful to me at an earlier time. We can't be responsible for another persons' behavior and we don't have to look to someone else to decide how we have to behave each day. I don't think AA existed when I was a teen and I certainly didn't know I could get help. Silence was best.

My parents wanted me to be tough and not complain. While playing basketball in Junior High School, I broke my nose and I learned not to tell my parents when I was hurt because they would pay no attention to it. I asked them to send me to a doctor a year later and they did but I chose not to have surgery. I also passed out when I fell off my bike but never told anyone. I tried very hard to please my parents.

Later while in high school, I had another boyfriend Pete who was very nice to me. He took me to the prom and I met and loved his family. His niece was named after me, Elizabeth. My full name is Elizabeth Scott Howe although I was nicknamed Scottie. Pete was like my best friend and we went our separate ways when he came to camp to work at the Aerie Campground one summer. I wanted to bum around with my friends there and he met a girl he liked. It worked out well and he is still a great friend and a super dancer.

Some of my time was spent at Judy's house where her brother Skip taught us how to shoot the basketball. He was a high school star and several of us girls asked his Mom for a souvenir and she gave each of us one of his socks. I kept mine for a long time. My friends and I never missed a high school game and Skip later went on to play with the Boston Celtics. Many years later I told Skip I had kept one of his socks around awhile and he laughed and said his mother had handed out a few but he didn't know I was one of his lucky fans. My practicing basketball in the summer helped me win a spot on the high school All Star team. We played other schools in the area and I liked the game and the orange slices handed out at half time. I played forward and was not the best player by any means but it was fun and I was awarded one of two letter sweaters that year. Bonny won the second one.

Mom would often attend the annual teacher's convention and we would have a sitter. The week that she was gone I was always anxious just waiting for her to come home. She was absolutely thrilled one year when the meeting was held in New York City for she rode in a taxi with author, Robert Penn Warren, and had the opportunity to speak with him. We watched television as she waved to us from the "Today Show" with Dave Garraway from Rockefeller Center. She had a wonderful time and when she returned home she brought me a new very stylish skirt and matching sweater with a pair of knee high socks. All the rage, the miniskirt was the stylin' way to go. I loved the green color and it fit beautifully but I was called into the principal's office and told not to wear it to school again. Earlier I had been voted "best figure" in a school yearbook and I was hugely embarrassed about it. I didn't want anyone looking at me and for some reason I didn't even think that the skirt would attract attention. I didn't wear the outfit to school again and am happy now to think that I may have worn the first miniskirt to Old Town High.

As I got older I would try to pour my father's liquor down the sink and confront him telling him he was an alcoholic and needed help. Being the oldest child I felt I had the responsibility to protect my mother and my siblings although I didn't think Dad ever physically abused them.

He would scream at me calling me names. While we were in the kitchen one day he called me a slut and I don't even think that we were arguing at the time. I asked my mother what that word meant and she told me he didn't mean it but didn't tell me what it meant.

Mom once asked me if I thought she should leave Dad. I said yes, brother Jim said no. She finally left him and he was shocked, just couldn't believe it. She was back with him after a month apart. Mom was very surprised and maybe a little hurt when I told her she was like Edith on the "Archie Bunker Show." I thought she was like the subservient character on television. Maybe she was afraid of Dad, too. I later became just like her in my relationship with my husband.

Our family attended a party at Kenner's camp at Howard Pond and Donna was with us, having come down to Hanover from Old Town for the weekend.

After the party as we started to leave for our camp, Dad decided to sleep in the road and Mom was frantically trying to get him up. She was eventually successful and they headed home to camp.

Donna and I and two of our male friends started to walk to camp and it was pitch black outside. We laughed and joked part of the way to our camp and then returned to get their car at the Kenner's camp. Dad thought it had taken me too long to get home to camp. Right in front of my friends, he met me at the top of the camp stairs. He drew off and belted me in the face and I fell down the entire flight of stairs and tore my dress. I was stunned. That night he was sitting on the floor next to my bed at camp crying and asking for my forgiveness. I said I forgave him but I just couldn't. The next day another friend asked me what had happened to me. He said he could see a red hand print on my face and it was badly swollen. I didn't tell him. I spent the day sitting on my special rock down at the Ledges. I would sit there by myself for hours and speak with God. I prayed that things would get better. I did anything I could to stay away from my father. I smiled on the outside but was hurting on the inside. Really hurting. My self esteem was at rock bottom but hidden there once again by a good actress. It was important that I kept busy and school activities kept me involved.

I don't know how our junior and senior high school singing group was formed but I remember rehearsing on the stage in the junior high gym and at Jane's house. At first we named the group the "4 Sharps and a Flat" but settled on the "Sharps." The original group was Sue, Jane, Charlene, Bonny and me, with Jane and I alternating between second and third parts. Mrs. Wareing, Jane's mother, played the piano and we practiced together and sang several popular tunes in three part harmony: "Knock on Your Door," "Blue Moon," and "Book of Love" were a few. Sue's Dad got us our first real gig singing before his Rotary Club and we were busy in preparation. We wore full pink skirts with a black musical note on them with white shirts, sneakers and bobby socks. A highlight was winning a March of Dimes Talent Contest at the Brewer Auditorium. Students from schools in our area competed and I can still picture the packed facility. It was tremendous to win and we earned a television spot on the Jim Winters Show, a show on which I had danced a few times before. Some of us also participated in the Maine State Chorus. Our last performance as the "Sharps" on television was with Jane, Teresa and myself in celebration of Old Town's Bicentennial. We wore long prairie dresses and there were bonnets to match. Jane and her mother got into an argument because we had just had our hair done and Jane did not want to wear a hat. Jane won the argument and we were grateful we didn't have to wear those bonnets. The Sharp experience was just that, an experience. We had a great time.

My aspirations were low and I didn't think about my future. It seemed normal to me to get married and have kids and possibly become an artist. I had very limited exposure to future opportunities, but ironically I loved telling people about the great State of Maine. Eventually I did promote Maine for a living and loved it. My parents loved us all and I don't want to leave the impression that they were too tough on me. I felt a lot was expected of me and I had to do well in everything I did but that was my choosing. I was appreciative of the love of the arts they gave me and have benefitted by that throughout my life. It was because I loved them so much that I wanted to please them and make them happy. I never felt that they pushed me but I never learned to do things to please myself. I needed their attention and the best way to get it was to do well.

Scottie tap dancing in the Bethel Minstrel Show.

The Howe home in Bethel

SIX

BETHEL * HANOVER
My paternal grandparents
1955-1962

While Barb and I were in Rockland, brothers Jim and Bob spent a portion of their summers with our paternal grandparents in Bethel. Bumpa who got his nick name from me as I bounced up and down on his lap while we rode in the car, was Dad's father, Winfield Scott Howe. Grammie Blanche was Dad's mother and Lennie Bean Howe was his grandmother and she lived with them in Bethel and Hanover. Our drives to Bethel from Orono or Old Town always seemed to take a long time but it was a trip just over two hours. Our family was crowded amongst our pets in the car, suitcases of clothes and food, basically everything six people couldn't live without for a week or two.

    Cut wood was stacked up on the outskirts of the town of Bethel with the fresh smell of sawdust reminding me that we were in Oxford County. A series of John Deere advertising signs were placed along the side of the road. Commercial buildings were mostly on Main Street and the railroad tracks bisected the town. Located in western Maine, Bethel is a picturesque mountainous town that always had more winter snow than we did in the central part of the State. My grandparents had an annual fear that the Androscoggin River would flood the house in the spring when the snow melted as it had done in the past. Bumpa worked near his home at a wood mill and the shed attached to his Bethel home was filled almost to the ceiling with dowels and smelled like sawdust too, very good. The wood was used to heat the house. There was a vegetable garden and a field of flowers in back of the house. The last time my brother Jim and I spoke, he mentioned the rhubarb there. The house was sold many years ago and is now a filling station on the left hand side of Route 2 as you head to West Bethel and New Hampshire after the Bethel Village exits.

The house in Bethel was by the railroad tracks and Barb and I would sit on the front steps and watch the man on the rail push car push the lever up and down as he made sure the track was clear ahead of the train. We waved to the engineer and caboose man and they always waved back. We counted out-of-state license plates as the cars sped by on busy Route 2. Grammie's house was small with a porch across the front and hardwood floors throughout. A mirror faced steps leading upstairs and I would tap dance up and down the wooden steps enjoying the echo I created.

Grammie and her Irish Setter, Judy.

Judy was always excited to see us. Grammie Blanche loved her dog and would often say to her, "Bless your old heartie." She sometimes called me "Scootchie" and would say, "It's a beauteous day today."

Each year Bumpa was an organizer of the popular local Minstrel Show. It was a major production with his friend Mr. Interlocutor and others, friends all, in black face doing slap stick and vaudeville acts. The cast were talented towns people who sang, danced, told jokes and put on a great show. Bumpa was a joker and had a wonderful Maine sense of humor.

He just naturally made those around him laugh, with a word, a joke, or a wink. He was a big man, well known and liked by everyone. During that time each year, Mom and Dad would put me on a bus in Bangor and I would travel more than two hours to Bethel to dance in the show. It was a thrill for me. The next day I would visit Grammie's fourth grade classroom and because I was younger than those in the class, I felt very grown up.

Grammie was slender, tall to me then, and had pretty gray permed hair. She too had a great sense of humor. Her students loved her as did I. She always wore dresses and usually had a sweater on because she loved to knit and could make a sweater in a day. She was strict and spoke her mind and I always feared her when I thought of doing something wrong. Her standards were high. I tried to please her when it came to my classroom grades even though she lived away. My parents would call their parents every other week and she kept up with how we were doing in school. I respected her and didn't want to disappoint her in any way.

Five generations with Sid Howe front and center.

Lennie Bean Howe in front of the new house.

In the early 60s my grandparents moved to a new home they built not far from camp on Howard Pond Road in Hanover. They installed French doors moved from the Bethel home and transported a large secretary from one house to the other.

There was a screened porch on the back of the house and Bumpa had bird feeders outside. He could name the species that visited the feeder. He also had about a dozen chipmunks he had named and they would eat peanuts from his hand. I don't know how he identified one from the other but they became tame.

In Hanover the Howe family owned many acres of land and Bumper had a garden called a nursery down a dirt road just up from the house. There was also on his property a pump located in a tiny building the size of a walk in dog house where everyone came for spring water.

Our camp, less than a mile up the road from the new house, was always a very special family place. The wooden two story hunting camp was built around 1900 by my great grandfather and it is the oldest camp on Howard Pond. The camp was built along a cow path that led to a pasture and Howard Pond was several yards out from the building. The pond is a clear spring-fed actual lake that is 109 feet deep and holds trout and salmon. It is about three miles in circumference and new construction around the edge of the water was halted in the fifties leaving around sixty camps there. A dam was built to control the depth of the water and protect the camps and now the water comes up underneath our camp porch. For many years we stayed there with no kitchen and no bathroom. Before the outhouse was built, we would go across the road to the woods to the bathroom and wash dishes in a black sink in the living room. We used kerosene lamps for light and our time at camp was entirely for family interaction. There were no distractions like phones and televisions and we enjoyed spending time together. I loved the woods, the sound of waves washing up to the camp and the smell of pine. It was a relaxing fun place. We played Gin Rummy and Cribbage there, more of Bumpa's favorites. The camp always smelled of fresh baked goods as my two grandmothers brought filled minced meat cookies, rhubarb pie and other favorites from the house to the camp for the next week. Grammie had a vegetable garden between our camp and the Richardson camp next door and wild flowers grew everywhere.

From our dock I would watch Jennie who lived in the camp next to ours swim out to the big rock between our camps with admiration. I was too small to swim that far but later swam the three miles around the pond with Paul in a boat following. As a teen I spent time on the Kenner's boat, in the pond swimming, and water skiing.

Our Dad put a store in our grandparents' basement and put in a beach on the pond. Being an only child, Dad didn't have to do much to sell my grandparents on the idea but there went their retirement time. The Aerie Campground became a family business. Opening day was exciting as town people and families from around the pond came and enjoyed an outdoor barbecue. Although the campground received rave national ratings and had many repeat customers, it never became a money maker. Mom said that Dad was not a business man because he liked people and was more generous than he should have been. We met many great people at the Aerie. One of my college art professors from Cincinnati camped there without knowledge of my connection and a Game Warden from Lee and his family stayed there. He and his son went rock hounding and came back to the campground with a backpack full of tourmaline. Dad joined them and stayed up all night to guard their discovery until they could have it appraised and placed in a bank deposit box the next day. After returning to the mine and finding a little more the next morning, they drove to Perham's

Gem Store in South Paris and the uncut gems were appraised at over $70,000. Soon the word was out and the mine site was overrun with fortune seekers. Dad had taken up rock hounding and gem cutting years earlier, long before his retirement as a State of Maine Fisheries and Wildlife biologist. He liked being a Maine Guide as well, but once he started cutting gems, he kept at it into his retirement. He sold gem stones and jewelry at the Aerie Campground store in Hanover, later moving the business to Belfast.

Seeing my summer time friends was great. At the Hanover camp we had a group, Ed, Jonathan, Brian, and me. We four would go to the fireworks in Rumford together and just hang out. Ed had a special clearing near his camp where we would put up paper targets and target shoot. One day a bullet ricocheted off a rock and bounced back hitting Ed in the leg. Fortunately he was O.K. but I never went shooting with them again even though I loved to shoot.

That summer when I was fourteen we entered nearly every empty camp on the other side of the pond. We took a boat across the pond, moored and would just go in and look around and leave. Sometimes we would quickly smoke a cigarette, but we never touched anything and liked the adrenaline rush, the apprehension it caused. I was curious as to what other camps looked like inside and knew it was something we should not be doing. I had no idea it was breaking and entering and illegal until later. One day Jon and I had taken out a window to get into a camp when we heard a car in the distance coming down the camp road. We crawled out of the camp through our entry point, couldn't get the window back on and set it up against the camp, and took off running to the boat. Just after we started the engine and left shore, we noticed a woman lifting up the blind in the front window. That was the last time I went along. The boys eventually got caught but I never spoke with them about it for I had returned to Old Town then and I never heard the details.

SEVEN

WAR SEEPS THROUGH GENERATIONS
Families left destroyed
1944-1958

During that trip to Boston when I was fourteen, I had a rude awakening as I realized that Dad was living with visible burn scars on his face. I had never really thought about them. Two boys sitting behind us at the Red Socks game were talking about Dad and one said,

"Look at him," pointing to my dad.

"He looks like a wolf."

It hurt so much, but Dad didn't act like he heard the comment so I ignored it too. It was painful to think of how often Dad must have gone through something like that. I later told a friend of Dad's, Curt, the story and he related to me how much it hurt him when Dad was teased when they were both at the University of Maine following their time in the service. Curt thought Dad was very strong and brave and he admired him a lot.

Dad was burned in World War II while in Morocco, Africa. He was enlisted in the Army and served for just under two years as a sergeant in communications. He was twenty-two and one of six soldiers riding in the back of an Army truck. The truck had walls around its bed nearly six feet high. The vehicle exploded. Only three men escaped over the high walls of the truck and of those, only two survived. Dad didn't know how he ever got out of that vehicle. Both survivors were in critical condition. A nurse riding in a vehicle behind the truck threw her cloak around Dad and put out the flames that engulfed him. He had second and third degree burns over more than 50% of his body and spent two years in Valley Forge General Hospital in Pennsylvania. Mom told me how Dad didn't want her to see him, to see his face, but she persisted. Mom was Dad's fiancée at the time of the accident and she woke up in Rockland that night knowing that something had happened to him. She knew his mustache was gone, it had burned off. Dad's entire face, ears and hands were reconstructed, grafted from skin taken from other parts of his body.

Mom moved to Paoli, Pennsylvania, to be near the hospital and visited Dad when she could. When Dad was better he and my mother were married in Rockland when Dad had a special leave from the Army.

I was born in Phoenixville, Pennsylvania. On one of our visits to Dad at the hospital, well known celebrity Eddie Cantor spoke with Dad and held me as a picture was taken for a publication like "Parade Magazine." My Godmother was Jane Hamilton and her husband John was the head of the National Republican Party. I don't think I ever saw them beyond my first year. I have often wondered what part the war played in my Dad's drinking. He went through so much. It is unbelievable and unforgivable that men and women are fighting wars today and bringing home with them the emotional and physical scars of battle. Their families sometimes go through more than they can handle. Dad worked until retirement age even though he was on full disability for his adult life. One of Dad's doctors explained to Mom that Dad could have emotional pain and become an alcoholic or express his anger in other ways. I am not making excuses for him, only trying to understand it.

Dad prior to his injuries.

EIGHT

MOVING ON
My marriage and a new generation.
1960-1975

When Mom went back to teaching full time she became head of the English Dept. and didn't get involved in the politics. An avid reader and "news" watcher, she was all up to date on current affairs. She had headed up Brownie and Girl Scout troops, was a member of Our Neighborhood Club and was extremely active while raising four children. I don't know how she did it and admired her very much. She just didn't like to make waves at all. She was an outstanding teacher and enjoyed her senior high school students, passing up several offers to teach at the University of Maine. A very humble and bright woman, she graduated from Bates College at the top of her class and was always available to talk with us or any student. She could keep secrets. Brother Jim and I both had her for a teacher. For me, when I walked into the classroom, she was my teacher. Jim had a harder time accepting her in a different role and acted up more than once. Mom spoke to him about his behavior and he was much better.

What was happening to me? I was losing my confidence and was torn up with anxiety about my family. I finally got up the courage to speak to the guidance counselor at the high school and Mom walked by his office as I sat there crying. I never opened up about my family strife or my thinking of suicide. Years later a group of women (HPWATS) and I invited our guidance counselor to meet with us for breakfast in Portland, Maine, where he worked. He recognized all of us. It was an interesting meeting for we women asked him to tell us what we were like in high school. Guess what he said about me. He said I had so much anger in me he didn't know how I would channel it. Positively or negatively. He was pleased to see it had been positively. When asked, he said he knew my dad was an alcoholic but couldn't discuss that with me if I didn't bring it up. I never did. I didn't think anyone knew and felt that our family was the only one with a problem like my Dad. I also thought I was protecting Mom.

Grammie Blanche with Grammie Howe at camp.

Remember my concern about having finger prints taken? Throughout the years I would lie awake nights agonizing over my family and its problems.

The school board banned the novel, "Manchild in the Promised Land" by Richard Wright. I had read the book and suggested Mom teach it because it opened my eyes to the real world when I went to college in Cincinnati from small town Maine. The first year she taught it to some of her senior high school class students, the book was banned by the Old Town High School Board and I felt entirely responsible. Mom had to go before the board and justify her teaching the best seller to the students and she was horrified. She didn't sleep for three nights before her appearance because there was nothing worse for her than having to stand and speak to a group of strangers in a public forum. At the same time I wrote a letter to a popular Maine newspaper, the Maine Times and they printed a lengthy article supporting her and the book and rejecting all censorship. After that the other news outlets followed suit and the book was reinstated. Mom was dedicated to her teaching and in one class we critiqued, "Sgt. Pepper's Lonely Hearts Club Band" by the Beatles. Learning is easier when the subject is of interest and the class discovered that Mom was cool. She was also responsible for the senior plays each year and directed the "Octogenarian" which won the state of Maine championship.

At the end of my junior year I chose the college I wanted to attend. Dad said I could go anywhere I wanted and I chose the University of Cincinnati. They had a top rated art department there and I was interested in the work study program in the College of Art, Architecture and Design. After graduating from Old Town High School, I joked with Bumpa telling him I was worried about getting my luggage and me to the dorm. He told me not to worry, that I would meet a handsome, polite young man who would help me out. I boarded the plane in Bangor and changed planes in

Boston and I felt as though I were in a daze. I felt sick to my stomach. I was alone and it was only my second trip out of Maine. Another passenger and I had been issued the same seat number and we were told to sit together. He was that handsome young man that Bumpa had mentioned, another student heading to Ohio and Xavier University. He got me a cab, carried my luggage into the dorm, and took me out to see the view from Cincinnati's tallest building and to dinner at a first class restaurant that night. The next day we got together and walked around campus before my orientation program. At the function we freshmen were told we could not walk on campus unless we were in a group of five. There was a sexual predator on campus and several students had been raped. I was scared.

When I was at the University of Cincinnati, I was the only Freshman selected for the University Chorus. The tryouts were done on an individual basis and as the conductor played the piano I sang "Drink to Me Only With Thine Eyes" in a key just right for me. He had selected the song. I had never sung it. The conductor asked me several questions and then told me I had a beautiful voice. I was walking on a cloud but didn't know I had made the chorus until several days later. We sang with the Cincinnati Symphony Orchestra and I wished during the whole time someone I knew from Maine was there to hear it. It was spectacular and I will never forget the experience. Throughout my life I have felt that God had blessed me with a love of the arts.

I liked my art classes and did all right in college and was just learning and enjoying how to study when I began experiencing medical problems. One day while downtown with two dorm mates, we went into a music store and we were invited to hear Gene Krupa who was playing drums upstairs. I had major back and stomach pain on the way up the stairs and turned right around, headed outdoors and caught the bus back to the dorm.

I was then taken by ambulance to the hospital. I had to have surgery and left school so I could have it at home in Maine, a decision that I regretted for years. I just can't believe I missed Gene Krupa! Dropping out of college when you are enjoying it is devastating. It was an incredibly difficult time for me and I became increasingly depressed.

Bumpa with a Howard Pond salmon.

Bumpa and Grammie with a visiting dog in their new home in Hanover, Maine.

I moved to Hanover to live with my Grammie and Bumper after leaving college and I discovered there were dances at the Top Hat in Hanover, Maine and I was thrilled. The huge barn was filled every Saturday night with local residents, young and old. There was a great live band that played the most current music back to the Virginia Reel. Some people in their eighties danced square dances and pre teens and youngsters would join in. It was like one big family gathering. One night I saw a man there and thought he was handsome. I asked Margo, a friend of his to introduce us and in just a little less than a year we were engaged. It was very appropriate that he asked me to marry him in a car and put a diamond on my hand at the Top Hat. I was in heaven. At the end of the summer I moved back with my parents and soon learned that most of my friends had left Old Town.

It was New Year's Eve and as with all holidays I began to get apprehensive several days in advance. Holidays seemed like a day that lightning struck my father and he would drink all day and turn into a different person. It was becoming impossible to find the father I loved. That night he drove drunk which he did often, and he rode his snowmobile up and down icy, snowy Stillwater Avenue. He was barefoot. As he came into the house I had the phone in my hand to call the police. My mother said he would lose his job if I called so I put the phone down but Dad saw what I was doing and he pulled my arm up behind my back and I was down on the floor on my knees. I was crying. Mom and my brother Jim were hitting him over the head and begging him to stop hurting me. When he let go I ran for the door and brother Jim threw his allowance and his car keys into my pocket and I was gone.

If I could have seen my hands when I was driving, I know my knuckles would have been white. It was dark and I was so scared. I drove onto I-95 and got away from the house, away from my father. The snow banks on either side of the road threw the brightness of the headlights back at me and the pelting ice on the windshield froze as it hit. The hail was company. It had rhythm. I didn't turn on the radio in case an emergency vehicle came up behind me. I wanted to hear it. The road was slick ice. I could barely see. There were no cars on the road, only tractor trailer trucks. I was crying and after thirty slow miles I got off the highway and pulled into a roadside restaurant in Newport. Shortly after ordering my hot chocolate, a police officer came in and sat next to me at the counter. He said there was an emergency and I was to call home immediately. When I called, Mom answered and told me that the State of Maine had been declared a State of Emergency and that all drivers were mandated by the State to get off the road. The Newport officer suggested I stay in the Newport Inn. I stayed up all night never leaving a chair by the front lobby window, gagging on the smell of cigars being continually puffed by the night watchman. At dawn I was out of there.

I headed to my grandparents' house in Hanover and from there I phoned my fiancé Gary and he came right over. We decided then to get married in two weeks rather than wait for June. We didn't go back to Old Town until a few days before the wedding. Mrs. Wareing bought me my wedding gown and veil at a Bangor dress shop. Mom had arranged the entire wedding and reception in two weeks. She even wrote the invitations out by hand. Friends brought food into the house for the reception following the service. The ceremony was in the Old Town Methodist Church at seven in the evening and it was lovely. Jane was my maid of honor, Doug the best man, and Dad was sober and walked me down the aisle. I was nineteen.

The first few years of marriage for me were good. The very first night I tried hard to put an appetizing first meal on the table but felt in a daze, being married, and tipped over Gary's glass of milk which landed up in his plate. The steak, potatoes and peas were covered with milk. It took me awhile to adjust to working as a waitress, keeping up the house which had a couch, chair, and bed, no stove but a hot plate balanced on the ironing board, and having a meal on the table when he got home from the mill. I worked at the Silvertone Restaurant in Rumford where the customers were locals and executives from the paper mill. I met Mary there, a special friend today, fifty years later. We had some fun times with an emotional boss and his fiancée. I took a ribbing for being a newlywed and walking funny. I liked waitress work but didn't want to do it forever.

I think I followed in my mother's footsteps by trying to take care of my husband's needs, building him up and making him happy while setting aside my own feelings. After our first few months in an apartment in Rumford, we moved to a house and then back to an apartment in Old Town so that Gary could attend the University of Maine. I was offered a full scholarship to return to the University of Cincinnati which I declined. That had always been my greatest regret until I found a professional job I loved, but honestly I do still regret it. In those days the woman's place was in the home supporting her husband and his education was much more important. I worked to put Gary through college and graduate school. Divorce was rare then. In fact I can only think of two girls I had known growing up whose parents had divorced.

While in Old Town I got a job as a salesperson, accounts receivable clerk at Old Town Furniture Company. I stayed with that job until Gary finished school. During his time at the University we had many parties and sometimes would have students from several different countries in our apartment. One of those students from Zambia, Geoff became a good friend and visited often. My parents invited us to their home for Sunday dinner and my siblings were also at the table with us as Mom served fried chicken. We all heard this crunching and Geoff was eating the whole chicken, bones and all. We tried not to laugh and got through the meal but afterwards I spoke to Geoff about it and he explained how great marrow is for your body and your teeth. We taught him some of our customs as he taught us his. I must confess, though, I have never eaten a bone. Geoff on the other hand learned what an egg salad sandwich was. He thought it might be a hard cooked egg between two pieces of bread, and he also discovered that beer tastes better from a can. At first he always asked for a glass.

Gary was smart and spent the time needed for studying and was committed to doing well. When he was in his senior year doing an all-nighter studying for his Senior final exams, I woke up at 4:00 am. and I told him I was ready to go to the hospital. We were to have our first child thirty-six hours later. Rhonda Tracey was born and his first question to me was,

"Where do you want to send her to college?"

We were truly enchanted. She was beautiful with a little blonde hair and blue eyes. She was the largest baby in the nursery, and looked about a month old. It made me feel much less apprehensive handling her. Soon after Rhonda's birth Gary graduated and we lived at camp and at the Aerie Campground for a summer. Later on we moved to Bath, Maine. as Gary accepted a State of Maine job as a social worker there.

There were several children in the neighborhood that Rhonda played with and they were busy with birthday parties and gym sets. Rhonda and Lisa, a little girl next door, became friends and when Rhonda was about a year old, I noticed that she was sliding behind in her speech development. It was noticeable to me because up until that time she had seemed ahead of Lisa even though they were the same age. Earlier Rhonda had been sick with German measles. At another time she ran towards the road and didn't respond when I yelled her name. She just kept on going. I chased her to the side of the road and when I picked her up she jumped. She hadn't heard me. At twelve months she had an appointment with her pediatrician and I told him I was concerned."How many others in your family think she has a problem?" he asked rather righteously.

"None," I replied.

"Not even your husband?"

I responded no and the doctor said he thought I was an over anxious mother because nothing was wrong.

"She should be speaking twelve words at eighteen months," he told me.

Well, I went home and counted. Rhonda spoke just twelve words. I took her back to the doctor soon after that and asked for a hearing test. She was tested at the Pine Tree Society in Bath and found to have a moderate to severe hearing loss. She was placed in classes for speech therapy and learned to speak one word at a time. We could watch her progress in classes through a two-way mirror.

She was also fitted with hearing aids and introduced to the John Tracy Clinic Correspondence program and Gary spent hours teaching her how to pronounce her words. Her loss was severe enough that we were told she would probably be placed in a special school for the deaf but she was unbelievably smart and through her determination and a good school system, she graduated as a Presidential Scholar from a public school. A remarkable achievement.

Rhonda lives in Phoenix and loves the Southwest and has been at the same company there for several years. The company provides services to the disabled. She is extremely independent, cares for three rescued feral cats that she has tamed, and lives alone. Best of all she has some very nice close friends and she does a lot for other people. She is sweet, temperamental, giving, moody, smart and loving and a NASCAR fan and rodeo volunteer.

Robert Michael was born at the Brunswick Hospital when Rhonda was eighteen months old. We were both thrilled to have a second child. After more than twenty-five hours in labor, just at a shift change, Rob decided to arrive. Gary was with me and rushed into the hall yelling for a doctor. Two nurses came into the room and told me I had to hold the baby in for there were no doctors in the hospital. I kept saying,

"I have to push."

They told me that it would rip me too much if I did. So…we waited and when the doctor arrived I was put under. I do remember the doctor pointing to Rob letting Gary know he had a boy. We were thrilled. Robbie spoke early on and was soon interpreting and communicating for Rhonda. Sometimes he could understand her when I couldn't and he would help me understand her. He is sensitive, precocious, intelligent, giving, and loving. He always had a mature wit and sense of humor which he uses to his advantage. He has the unique gift of being able to make others laugh. One afternoon we took Rob and Rhonda to see "101 Dalmatians." Rob was about two and sat on my purse on my lap so he could see the screen and he laughed throughout the movie. The audience spent the time laughing at him. His baby laugh was contagious and he was the star of the show. Robbie and Rhonda were very special brother and sister. They are today. Rhonda protected Rob and Rob guided Rhonda.

NINE

SOCIAL CHANGE
Total Confusion
1960-1972

There was political turmoil throughout the sixties. The Height Ashbury section of San Francisco had become a scene filled with flower people, peaceniks and those ignoring the conventional norms of the country. Thousands of young people went to California as a way to reject society, show individual creativity and discover new ways to live off the land. They had ideas of complete freedom while at the same time others their age were fighting for the country's freedoms in Vietnam. The country was torn in two. Too many men went to war. Too many men did not return home. A medical condition kept Gary home and we were thankful for that, but sadly we both lost men we knew in the war. It was an extremely tumultuous time.

The woman's movement was gaining strength and although I didn't pick up a placard and march. I understood the female's right to demand equal pay and to no longer be dependent upon her husband. It was a major change in thinking for up until that time women were expected to be somewhat subservient to their spouses, the bread winners.

A few years later while working at the Chamber of Commerce in Rockland, a male employee in my office, hired by me, introduced me to a representative of a large Portland development firm. As I shook his hand he said, "I knew they hired a new executive but I didn't know it was a per…per…person."

He wanted to say woman but he caught himself mid-sentence and it shifted to person. I shook his hand and was most business like trying not to laugh. Several months later he asked me if I remembered our introduction and I told him yes. We both had a good laugh. It was a difficult time in our society, for men and women alike. Most people were aware of women's desire for independence and equality and that it was difficult to attain. When women felt they were worthy of power in their careers and they worked hard, they were successful at getting it to some extent.

Unknowingly I sat at a table at the Rotary Club which had always been occupied by the same four men. When they arrived one of them said,

"She's just like one of us. She's like a man with her own power," and he pulled up a fifth chair for me. Another business man I dated said he was first attracted to me because of my power. I just didn't know how to feel about either comment. I knew how to get things done but felt much of it had to do with who you knew. I asked a friend, a director how he would take being called powerful as a female and he said it was a huge compliment. I truly didn't know how to take it.

When women felt they had to cease playing the subservient role at home, the change frustrated their husbands although change in their homes may have been achieved easier than in their jobs. Some women felt they had to act like a man to succeed in their careers. A woman sat down in front of my desk in my office and shouted to me that she was f…… sick of the city. She felt she had been overlooked for a number of positions and the recognition she deserved. I agreed with her. She was puzzled that I was the first woman to be invited into the Rotary Club and she was not. She even pounded on my desk as she said it. I explained to her that trying to act tough and behaving like a man would not work. Things did get better for her when she just began to be herself. She was searching for power. Marriages failed during those difficult times of transition and what many had known as a core family unit became a single parent home. Women then worked because they needed income and many were thrust out on their own. The woman who came into the office had a successful career and was able to manage family and work together. She was highly admired in the community.

Music was huge in the 50s and 60s and those our age had stacks of LPs. Our collection of records included "Hair," " Jesus Christ Superstar," and the groups "Moody Blues," and "Journey." I wore the tie dye shirts and blue jeans and went barefoot for most of one year. My Nana was horrified when a friend of hers offered to buy me a pair of shoes. I felt somewhat embarrassed for my grandmother but loved the small sense of rebellion walking down the street in Rockland smoking a cigarette with my long hair down almost to my waist. The kids were babies and I wasn't working at the time. I didn't really want to step into hippyville but enjoyed a touch of acting like a young person of the 60's, which I was. There was social upheaval during that period unlike any period since. For a time I wore two maternity dresses repeatedly, they were all I had. I went two years in Bath rarely going anywhere except to visit neighbors, and suffered with a major case of athletes' foot from the one pair of white loafers I wore without socks for over a year. I remember the look on the face of the specialist in Lewiston as he examined my bloody feet.

"Is that athletes' foot?" I asked.

He just shook his head back and forth and said yes.

When first married we had very little money as did many couples our ages. I found a dollar one day and had a great time looking for something to spend it on. I found a rod-like contraption that holds an iron cord up and away from the ironing board and thought it was a unique invention. When I showed Gary what I had bought with the money he just laughed. Guess it was funny, but I sure didn't think so at the time. The only other item I bought for myself then was a three dollar pair of figurines that reminded me of Rhonda and Rob. They were on display in a store window I walked by on my way to work. The pants on the little boy were falling down in back as Rob's were at his age. I still have the items on display in our bathroom.

I didn't want to go back to work as it seemed like a long time since I had been employed, but Gary really wanted me to find employment and we needed the money. I started working nights at the Mart in Brunswick and was soon managing the lunch counter. I liked it. One night when I got home earlier than usual, Gary was sitting on the couch with his arm around our next door neighbor, my friend Karen. He apologized and said nothing happened between them. I cried all night. It was such a shock to me. In just minutes I had lost my feeling for him. The trust was gone.

Karen moved away, divorced her husband who was in the service overseas at the time, and returned to her home state, Louisiana. I continued my job at the Mart until we moved to New Orleans. I didn't work in the day time before the kids started school but did teach a group of children art lessons. One of them won first place in the statewide "Bangor Daily News" Art Contest. Although we had moved away shortly before the contest the student's mother called me to let me know her daughter had won. Her parents and the student were pleased and so was I.

The perception and utopian views of the hippy movement were short lived and not appealing to me as drugs overtook it in a big way. Many of us tried grass at the time as I did at my husband's urging, but I was uncomfortable with it. I didn't like the feeling of being out of control. I also had a father's example of what alcohol could do and was fearful of drugs and alcohol. The connection I had with my husband was lost when I realized he was unfaithful. It was the last thing I wanted to hear and I was probably the last one to realize it. We never spoke about it, I just blocked it out, or so I thought.

To get away, I flew with Rhonda when she was about four to Arlington, Virginia, to visit with my sister who worked at the Pentagon. Barbie had two children, Elizabeth and Jacqueline and they were about four and two, the same ages as my children. Barb was putting up a playpen in front of her door at night so she could hear when her husband got home for she knew he had a girlfriend and she was extremely unhappy. She also had some bruising from him hitting her. In addition to all of that, Liz had come home from the babysitter with bruises on her thigh and Barb wanted to get out of there. Not too long after my visit, she and her husband divorced and she and the girls moved back to Maine. They stayed with our parents until they could move out to an apartment on their own. They found housing and lived there until Barb bought her own home on French Island in Old Town. She was happy and comfortable there and her neighbors watched out for her and were very caring and good to her.

Our loving sister, Barbara Jean Howe Urtecho

At the time of my visit to Washington, Barb and I had made an appointment to go to the Corcoran Gallery of Art in Washington, D.C. It was a cab ride and near the White House. Jim Harris had been my art teacher when I was thirteen and fourteen and he took me into the classes he taught at the University of Maine. When Barb and I visited him, he was the curator of the Corcoran Gallery of Art in Washington, D.C. There had been a major article about him in the "Washington Post" and "Time Magazine" that my mother had mailed me, so Barb and I looked him up. When we walked into the gallery, a guard did not take his eyes off us until we told him we had a meeting with Mr. Harris. He quickly ushered us into a private office. Mr. Harris asked about an art project we had worked on the last time we were together which had been more than ten years prior. I was astounded he remembered me. During our meeting in his office, he offered me a one woman show at the Corcoran. He wanted someone from Maine and said that a young woman would be fantastic. Best of all, he knew my work which gave me confidence. It truly didn't mean much to me at the time, being unfamiliar with galleries and the art world, but I did follow through and started a twelve canvas project for him as he requested. During the third painting for his series, I nearly miscarried Robbie, and had to spend time in bed. To do art as I wanted to do art was all consuming and with family it was difficult to dedicate my whole self as I would have wanted, to become successful. I did not touch art for another twenty or more years and I never got back the freedom to express myself on canvas with the freshness I had when I was younger. Mr. Harris is the most inspirational person I have ever met. I went home and got my frustrations out with paint. Barbie did too.

I can still picture Rob and Rhonda red-faced as we drove to New Orleans from Bath in August in the early 70's with no air conditioning in the car. Karen had encouraged Gary to do his grad studies in Louisiana. I don't think either of us realized how bad the heat would be. Gary had been offered a full scholarship for a Masters Degree in Social Work Administration at Tulane University with a commitment to work in the state of Maine afterwards. After he checked in at the school, we headed to the Holiday Inn off I10 near the airport in Metairie and we stayed there for the night. The next day we found a new second floor apartment on Houma Blvd. and we slept two nights on the carpeted floor until the moving van arrived with our things. We rented furniture and we settled in.

Eventually we became familiar with the French Quarter, the greatest party place in the world for college students. We were invited to Mardi Gras by a priest in Gary's class and went to his church which was enclosed by a fancy rod iron fence. Being separated from the huge crowd made it wonderful for there were tables set up with all the food you could imagine and the amenities of home were available away from the people watching the twelve hour parade. We caught many beads thrown from the floats passing by and used them to make a bead curtain.

TEN

HPWATS
My BFF's
1962-present

After Gary graduated we moved back to Maine arriving in Old Town on Christmas Day. The air was cool and brisk, the roadway wet, and we were home. Maine was welcoming. When we drove into the State I felt tremendous happiness, joy and relief to be home. The trees on either side of the road were snow covered and the sun streaking through the branches made them sparkle. Nana, Grammie, and Bumpa were at the house in Old Town and my brothers and sister were there too. Food and laughter awaited us and a beautifully decorated tree sat in the living room. Best of all, Dad was sober. Anytime I have been asked since which was my favorite Christmas, I tell of that one. It was the last time we were all together.

These men represented Rockland in the 1898 war with Spain, sparked by the exploding of the battleship Maine off Havana harbor. Our home in Rockland was once owned by Mervin ap Rice, second from left and John Bird on right was a lawyer and Papa Bird's brother.

Nana found a nice house in Rockland that had belonged to a friend of hers who had died. The drawers were full, paintings hung, and furniture in place. There were thirteen fully furnished rooms, four fireplaces and history galore. We were the third family to live in that home. The first was Atty. Nathan Farwell who was at one time in President Lincoln's cabinet, the apRice family, and our family. With dark woodwork, wood floors and oriental carpets, it was similar to Papa's house. I thought, this is Christmas for the rest of my life. I still think of that…sometimes. We refurbished each room stripping any painted woodwork or floors and replaced worn wallpaper with new paper that looked like it could have existed in the 1800's. The house was beautiful with interesting features and an octagonal library with three shelves filled with almost one thousand books around all eight walls. The library fireplace had four foot high andirons and a built in china cabinet, one of several in the house. There were four fireplaces in the house. We entertained the Governor of the State of Maine on two occasions, and Caroline Kennedy in that house. I had attended my first Democratic caucus and was voted the Chairman of the Democratic Party in Rockland. My interest was short-lived as political science was Gary's interest, not mine. I still cared for my husband. Once the feeling of love is gone, though, there is nothing. There was nothing.

In the early seventies, soon after we moved to Rockland, I faced depression for the second time, the first being after I left college with back problems. I knew I had to do something to help myself when I was driving down Interstate 95 and didn't want to go home and face Gary. As I drove under each overpass, I wanted to speed up over 70 mph and turn the wheel and hit the huge cement barrier. I was incredibly unhappy and I still remember picturing my kids. I never could have left them and with anxiety, fear and dread I would put on a happy face and return home.

My solution to begin to get beyond the depression was to reach out to friends and I invited twelve former high school friends to the house. As it often is when we get together with old friends, our roles with each other were the same and we spent most of the weekend laughing. It was wonderful for me and although I gave the impression that all was well with me, it wasn't. Things did start to look up though. My friends and I still meet every year and most of the time we have our reunions at our family camp in Maine. Each person has contributed to the group in their own way and some of us have been friends since we started kindergarten together and we all graduated from Old Town High School in 1961 or 1962. Carole named our group the Howard Pond Walking and Talking Society, (HPWATS) and we have been meeting for fifty years.

At camp, we "girls" spent one summer with pig faces we wore that were a pair of sun glasses connected to a pig nose mask. Water could be squirted from the nostrils from a side pump. I remember a couple of the women talking about a couple of policemen laughing at them when they used the pig noses in a Burger King parking lot in Farmington on their way to camp from Old Town. Can you imagine a couple of gray haired ladies chasing and squirting each other with a pig nose? One year we competed to see who could find the best squirt gun. We blew bubbles, locked the door when some of us were outside in the pouring rain, and had about a ten year period of pranks. Our early years were filled with reminiscing about other friends, school and younger times. The next segment of our times together could be described as prank and practical joke time. Now we are in a mellow stage. We go to bed early and truly appreciate one another.

Our best prank happened during a fun-filled weekend at camp when we were in our fifties. By midnight we had all settled down in the beds or on the floor in our sleeping bags. There was a loud banging on the front door and a man's voice rang out,

"Diane, Diane, are you in there?"

When the women peeked out the window they saw a man with a heavy jacket and baseball cap on. They didn't turn on the outside light and it was difficult to see out, it was so dark. He continued shouting, sounded very drunk, and everyone was panicked. Everyone except Donna and me who slept on the porch. We had planned the joke earlier with Jennie, a friend in town. The camp was in utter chaos. The women had sleeping bags pulled up to their armpits as they tumbled together to head up the stairs. Brave Nancy held the outside door and stood leaning against it in her underwear trying to keep the bad man out. I pretended to call the Sheriff and tried desperately not to laugh. The man outdoors poured some water on one of the coolers and everyone thought he was throwing up. A few of them expressed their concern,

"I sure hope that's not on my cooler!"

Then pebbles flew and we could hear them bouncing off the roof. Sue screamed that she was getting a knife having told the man many times,

"There is no Diane in the camp,"

and Bonny suggested he might be saying dying instead of Diane. After hearing the word knife, the man staggered up the outside stairs to the road and left, driving very erratically as his every move was reported from Janet who was watching out from the upstairs window. Nurse Janet was very concerned that he was on the road in that condition. Sue stated emphatically that she would not stay in the camp again until we had a lock, no several locks, on the front door. I don't think any of us got any sleep that night. Donna and I because we were laughing so hard while trying to be quiet and the others because of sheer fear. My cheeks hurt from laughing quietly.

The next noon as everyone was sunbathing on the float, a voice shouted,

"Diane, Diane, are you in there?"

Well, I have never seen so many mouths open at the same time. Each of the women seemed in shock as they turned around and it finally dawned on them that the man was their friend Jennie. She had worn her husband's clothes and changed into a man for that one night. Excellent job! I don't know if they will ever forgive Donna and me.

Jane

Carole, Scottie and Ann trying out the infamous pig noses

Now we are in our mellow, loving stage and we have saved money on psychiatrists as each of us continue to give sound advice, at least we think so, as we all go through life.

We are always changing, though. Donna was thrilled when she noticed I had some chin hairs. She had some too just like most of us. When I jokingly acted like I didn't think her bringing it up was appropriate she said,

"They only show because you are sitting in the sun."

Sure, Donna. Good try.

We have talked about our hair thinning, nails curling under, wrinkles, loose skin and double chins amongst other things. A change over the fifty years we have been meeting is with our boobs, once cupcake like with a cherry on top and now like two loaves of bread. Somewhere along the way some of our bikinis became bathing suits, skirt style. It has been a delight to learn so much women stuff from a loving group of friends. They all mean a lot to me, more than they will ever know.

HPWATS
Front row: Carole, Nancy, Janet
Middle row: Cassandra, Scottie, Gail, Sue,
Standing: Bonny, Donna and Helen

ELEVEN

DEEP SORROW
My life crashes.
1972-1975

We continued to appear as a happy couple but I was absolutely devastated inside. During one of the parties we hosted with Gary's office staff, I spoke with one of his bosses and told him that things seemed good but I felt something bad was about to happen. In less than a months time he brought that conversation back to me. Right after speaking with him, I turned to go into our library and Gary was on the sofa with his arm around a woman there. I turned and walked out. I felt so trapped! I never had any money at all and handed over any check that I made at work to Gary without cashing it. That was the way he wanted it and I was beginning to become afraid of him so I complied. I didn't want any conflict and agreed to do what he wanted. If I wanted to buy something I had to ask him for the money. He had control. It was awful. A friend of mine told me she didn't like coming over to my house anymore because the tension was thick. I still didn't know how I could get out of the marriage but I was determined then that I would do it.

Falling into a dependent role in a relationship happens gradually. In my case, I tried too hard to please my husband and lost sight of myself as an individual. I asked his permission for everything and thought he would be angry if I didn't. Had I known the repercussions a house of stress can have on children, I never would have stayed in the marriage as long as I did. I think we all had to read Gary's actions each day as I had done with my father, to decide how to behave that particular day. Since Gary and I didn't fight openly in front of the children I didn't think they were being hurt. I have learned since that they knew and understood much more than I thought they did.

About a week after Gary's office party, Rhonda, who was five, came to me as I was doing dishes and tugged on my skirt. She had taken a Christmas gift upstairs to our tenant, Edith, and came back to tell me Edith had a funny dress on. I didn't think much of it until about an hour later the phone rang and it was a friend of Edith's asking me if I had seen her. I told her I would go upstairs and check on her and call her back.

When I walked into Edith's kitchen upstairs through the heavy door between our section of the house and her apartment, there were black cobwebs across the kitchen and living room ceilings. Edith was lying on the floor. A meal she had prepared was sitting on the kitchen counter with a sliced apple all shriveled up, and her two cats had become wild. I reached down and touched Edith's back and felt charcoal. Her hair looked way shorter than usual and stood out on her head. The television was on and I thought maybe she had been electrocuted. I ran back downstairs, yelled for Gary and dialed 0 for the operator. I told the operator I thought Edith may have been electrocuted and may be dead. Help arrived quickly. Edith had died although it was difficult for me to accept that.

A kindergarten teacher heard about the fire from her police scanner and came right to our house to watch Rhonda and Rob.

She was an angel. Edith had a skull fracture which was unusual and the investigators thought it was foul play. I was questioned about an hour in the kitchen.

That same night the woman who sold us the house and initially rented to Edith came to our house and explained to the officials that the fracture had come from an accident Edith suffered while in the Army. Plus, four thousand dollars had been found in the bureau in her apartment, which the investigator who questioned me was happy about. I had been a suspect and didn't even know it. Apparently Edith had been drinking, dropped a lit cigarette on her chest, and was wearing a polyester fabric that gave off poisonous fumes. She had taken some steps and fallen. I was shown the melted spots on the carpet where the melted fabric had dripped onto the floor and she had tried to escape. It was just awful.

Eventually, I remembered that six days earlier I had heard the fall but thought one of the kids had fallen out of bed and when I checked, saw that they were asleep. I never thought of checking upstairs. I guessed it was a noise outdoors. Edith's body burned a hole in the floor right over the kids' bedroom and I have given thanks many times that they were not harmed.

Less than two weeks after Edith's accident, my Mom called and told me she had terminal lung cancer. I rocked back and forth as I sat on the floor and was completely dazed and bawling. Mom was 53. It was such a shock I couldn't do a thing and for the first time I took medication to calm me down. Mom, bless her, never stopped teaching. She taught me strength, faith, and compassion as she lived it during her life and through her illness. I loved her more than I can ever express and miss her unconditional love to this day. I drove to Bangor nearly every weekend to be with her during the last two years but didn't know I was going up for her final 48 hours. I called and asked if she wanted me to visit and for the first time she gave me a definite yes. I cried all the way there. I knew something was different about this trip. When I arrived she was in good spirits and we played a word game Boggle and she beat me as usual. In the middle of the night I heard her coughing and checked on her and she said she wanted to go to the hospital. Dad was there but he was drunk so I called an ambulance and rode with her. Dad arrived at the hospital to join us about twenty minutes later.

We had a few hours to spend with Mom and when brother Jim arrived he and I were sitting on each side of her and holding each hand. The nurse came in and asked us to leave for a few minutes so they could change the bed. I asked the nurse,

"Do we have to?"

I felt our leaving her would give Mom a chance to leave us. Mom died when we left her. She was fifty-five. Just before Mom's funeral, everyone gathered at Mom and Dad's house on Stillwater Avenue and Gary just left. He said nothing. He walked out the door and was gone for Mom's funeral week. My brothers were my rocks as I sat through the funeral with Rob on my lap and Rhonda by my side. I later heard that Gary had gone to a party at a camp with a woman.

Mom's funeral was a private immediate family affair as she wished. The minister read the "Twenty-Third Psalm," A. A. Milne's "Vespers," and Eugene Field's "Wynken, Blynken and Nod" and "Little Boy Blue." As children she taught us Bible verses and children's poems. I love the poems and verses today as much as I did then. I was crying on the outside and screaming on the inside. Get me out of here! I can't take it any more.

Mom's graduation day from Rockland, Maine.

TWELVE

GOD WITHIN US

Throughout my life if I had been asked, "Who are you closest to?" I would have answered, "God."

Mom took us children to church from the time we were youngsters until we could make our own choices about our spiritual life. She sat with brother Jim on her lap as he cried each time the organist played. He was moved deeply by music even at the age of two. God was within us. Always. I was comforted by Him and many of my prayers have been answered over the years.

FROM ONE WHO WAS QUITE ILL

To those who sent cards__
May I say thank you.
Cards have a way of leaping space--and time--
Reaching out to clasp hands,
Saying, "Wasn't it fun? Remember When...?"
Cards make a mockery of separation from the past

To those who sent plants
Many thanks!
Plants are a tie-in to life.
Plants say, "See and smell and touch
The world is beautiful- reach out, touch me,
Live me now!
Plants are earth and sky, sun and water--
Indoors they bring the world close.

To those who sent gifts--
My thanks.
You Know
Love is made of little things
Like sighs, and fingertips, and smiles
And time spent in preparation.
Love is always someone else.

To you who sent prayers--
And maybe thought I didn't know--
You gave me breath
And carried me on a blanket of love.
You have belief--
The most awesome gift of all.

Dorothy F. Howe
Our Mom

    I have always felt that the formal religions are not necessary for everyone for God can come into our hearts anytime and any place. We simply have to ask. During the summer following my senior year I worked as a waitress at the Lighthouse Restaurant at Pemaquid Point on the Maine coast. Five of us waitresses lived together in a camp, just a parking lot away from the actual lighthouse. While there I saved every penny for college and since we had afternoons off, I would get on my bathing suit after work and run on the huge rocks on shore, trying to avoid the cracks between them. The ocean waves were sometimes grand, absolutely spectacular, and I found a boulder with an indentation on the top and would often sunbathe there. As I was relaxing there one afternoon a huge wave came crashing over me and pulled me out to sea, feet first. I remember thinking,

" I am going to die."

I was being pulled into a bright whirlpool-like bright white light tinged with blue.

It was blinding but I felt euphoric and happier than I ever had been. Someone was inside at the end of that cone-shaped light and although I was tempted I resisted going into it and the figure disappeared. I reached down and held firmly onto some seaweed or something attached to the rocks under the ocean water. It held me as the water rushed out over me. A man on shore, Dr. Crozier from Philadelphia ran down to help me and I was fine. I have never feared dying since that day.

When Mom was sick she explained how she had felt like she was floating above everyone in the hospital room and that she would hear their conversations. Later while hospitalized for her two final days of life, I phoned her each morning at eight. The first call was an opportunity for her to explain,

"There is a bright white light in the corner of my room and someone is motioning for me to come."

She would describe what she was feeling. The next morning I called and she asked,

"Do you remember my telling you about a light?"

I said yes and she said,

"The light was Dad and he was standing by a lamp in the corner of the room."

I didn't know if she meant her dad or my dad, but she seemed relieved and relaxed that she had figured it out.

It has always felt to me that these experiences had come from being close to dying and that God was with us until our choice to leave or to stay was made.

THIRTEEN

LOST FEELINGS
Broken vows
1974-1984

I was talking to a neighbor Elaine, and she asked me if I was interested in working for the Chamber of Commerce in Rockland. I asked her what the Chamber did, and she explained the job to me. I had finally told her that I was in an unhappy marriage and with both kids in elementary school, it was time for me to do something with my life. Elaine was very encouraging. Her husband was involved with the city and I felt that the people at City Hall who knew me as a child would support me. I applied and made Chamber work a twenty year career. I worked at the Rockland Chamber for a couple of years as an assistant and left for a year to work in a lawyer's office. There was no comparison in atmosphere. I needed the hustle and bustle of the Chamber and the noise of people coming and going.

The Howe family at camp. Dad, Scottie, Jim, Barbie, Bobby. Notice how we are all hiding our Howe chins?

It saddened me to listen to the lawyers talking about how stupid women were not to leave their abusive husbands knowing I was one of them. When an opening came up for the Executive Director position at the Chamber I applied and had my first opportunity to encourage others to work together to improve our city. It was an exciting undertaking and I absolutely loved it. It was a good fit. Not only was I promoting Maine but I was also given tons of responsibility and I thrived. We were involved in a downtown revitalization project at the time and it became a turning point for Rockland. No longer was it a town of a smelly fish processing plant. The company had closed. I took groups of business owners to Portsmouth, New Hampshire and Newburyport, Massachusetts by motor coach and they came back to Rockland with color schemes for their store fronts and ideas for the public areas. They learned about traffic flow, pedestrian walkways and listened to speakers who had already made improvements to their cities. The trip was incredibly successful and even those I never thought would put a penny in to change things, did. During the next several decades, Rockland got cleaned up, became a higher sales tax income area than its nemesis, Camden, and after a few years became the town with the most windjammers based on its coast. Rockland has done a complete turn around. It was the right time and I was the fortunate one to have been there at the beginning. I was also thankful to have worked with a dynamic city manager and Chamber of Commerce Board members. The improvements in that city continue today. Rockland is unrecognizable as the city it was when I lived there forty years ago.

My job offered me an opportunity to attend the Organization for Chamber Management Institute at the University of Delaware in Newark for a week for six summers. My classmates and I became wonderful friends and learned a lot from each other. The first year I attended I was built up to such a point that I felt giddy. I had never felt better about myself and others were coming to me for advice. What a high. Confidentially I spoke to a counselor while there and told him I didn't think my husband liked my becoming successful and he recommended some books for me to read through the winter, which I did. By the second summer when I went back I felt confident and by the third summer I felt strong. I continued there for three more years and for two years served as a class advisor.

When I returned home after each week away, Gary was hostile. I am not going into details but I realize that I will never be able to explain to myself why I never got help. Silence. I didn't want attention brought to my children and with my public activities felt it would be. I didn't want to hurt Gary or have others hurt him because of me. I didn't want him to lose his job or want others to know I was unprepared or too weak to go it on my own and leave him. I was without a penny, insecure and afraid and the only way out was to let the secret out and keep busy.

I soon became involved with the local schools Self Assessment Program and those in the group encouraged me to run for the School Board. I was committed to continuing the work of the committee and decided to become more involved. As part of that process I participated in a Candidates' Night. I waited and waited for Gary to return home from his "meeting" in Bangor so he could take me. It was an important event for me and I hoped for his support. He never showed up. I did well with the press interviews which were broadcast, and was elected with the most votes as a member of the S.A.D. 5 School Board. I didn't think Gary was happy about it but went on later to again become the highest vote getter for a second term. Public service was gratifying to me and I encouraged anyone with interest to give it a try. To me it was like a free education. I learned all about the community, how it worked, about goals and budgets and met many interesting people. On boards, I tried to speak only when I felt it was important and learned to read each member and their role in the group setting. Group dynamics was fascinating to me. Eventually my career became who I was.

I can honestly say I don't know what happened to Gary. He changed tremendously and I did not know him anymore. He had become a very different person and I was frightened to be near him. The last time when we were fighting upstairs in our bedroom Rob yelled upstairs, "Cut it out!"

Gary stopped just long enough for me to finally get past him and run downstairs. I comforted Rob and he asked me if we were going to get divorced. I said yes. A teacher renting our upstairs apartment at that time told me she almost called the police. I told her I was glad she didn't, but oftentimes after that wished she had. Gary went to counseling and I was eventually asked to join him. Gary and I had been married eighteen years. By the time I left counseling after a year and a half I felt confident that I could manage by myself and with my income. I felt the counselor was extremely good and connected and I also knew that I had worked as hard as I could to save the marriage. I left the last session with a smile on my face, a sense of relief and my head held high. I filed for divorce.

Rob, Dr. Jackie, Liz and Rhonda in Rockland

FOURTEEN

BYE, BARB
BYE, DAD
Loss of unconditional love.
1983-1987

After nine years as the director of the Chamber of Commerce in Rockland, I went to the Greater Bangor Chamber of Commerce. I was interviewed by ten men which could have been intimidating but I was confident and very sure of my work. Soon I moved the one and a half hours to Bangor with the two kids, a dog and a cat with stuff packed to the roof of the car. I had made plans to meet the men with the moving van in front of our new house on West Broadway at 8:30 am. We ran out of gas in Hampden. Here I was going door to door very early in the morning trying to find someone who was up and who had a phone. The problem was solved and we were happy to move into our new house.

One of the advantages of living in Bangor is that sister Barbie lived nearby in Old Town and we could get together often and we did. We sometimes went out dancing or just sat around drinking coffee and talking sister talk.

Barb got sick. Very sick. I was in such shock that when Dad told me she had lymphoma I couldn't say a thing. I just couldn't believe it. She was too young and was given five years to live. Life seemed so unfair, I could not bear it. I wanted to die, too. I did what I could for her then but I was absolutely helpless and hopeless. She did much more for me. Her strength and ability to continue to do things for herself and her friends just amazed me. She worked throughout most of her chemotherapy and would joke about her chemo cut when her hair was short. She kept people laughing. During the five years of her illness, we became closer than ever and spent more time together than we ever had. The move to Bangor was one of the best things I could have done. Liz and Jackie, Barb's children were able to spend their Christmases in our home and spend time with Rhonda and Rob. This past Christmas, all four are now in their forties, they wrote on Facebook how much they enjoyed those years. We sang, we danced, and most of all, we laughed.

A few months before Barbie died, I finally convinced her to take a few days vacation with me in Quebec City, Quebec, Canada. She hesitated to go but once we hit the road she seemed fine. We spent the first day window shopping near the Chateau Frontenac when I opened up a door along a side street and started walking up some stairs to the second floor. Barb thought I was crazy and kept trying to pull me back downstairs by my sleeve. She didn't know how to read French and a sign outside the building read, "Hair Styling Salon." We got to the top of the stairs and everything was white, the furniture, walls, and even carpets, and we were ushered into separate rooms where we put on white robes. We didn't see each other until we both had completely new hairstyles. Barb's was punk and mine was cut up around my ears. New and different we were both thrilled. We couldn't stop laughing.

That night after dinner we went dancing in a large room connected underground to the hotel. I was asked to dance and Barb sat at the table. When I was escorted back to the table, Barb was on her way onto the dance floor with an attractive man. She whispered to me,

"Forget the note on the table."

The note at the table scribbled on a napkin said,

"It has been a long day and I am going to bed."

After dancing several dances she and her partner returned to the table. Barb pleaded with me to go out to breakfast with a group she had met. It was almost two in the morning and I told her I couldn't. I had to drive home the next day and get back to work, so we said our good-byes to our new friends.

The next morning we went to the hotel restroom together and I walked into the mens' room by mistake. There was a man standing in front of a mirror combing his hair. I got out as fast as I could and Barb had completely vanished. She was so shocked by her older sister. To add to that, on the way home we stopped for lunch at a gas station converted to a diner. The food was good and Barb paid the tab as I walked out front. She could keep an eye on me through two plate glass windows across the front of the building. There were old gas tanks covered by a large metal protective cover, like a roof, with lights underneath it. I wasn't standing out there long when I heard a buzzing sound and it felt like I had a mosquito fly into my ear. I was putting my head to one side and then the other hitting my head just above the ear trying to get the bug out. I was doing just what you do when you get water in your ear from swimming. I did not know that several people, so Barbie said, were watching me from inside and laughing. She didn't know what was going on with me. Just as Barb came out to go I realized that the florescent light bulb up over my head had a short and was making a hissing sound. It wasn't my ears at all. It wasn't a bug. Barb did think it was another ridiculous incident with her sister and I must admit, it tickles me to this day.

I was alone with Barbie at the Dana Faber Cancer Institute in Boston when her doctor asked me out into the hall and told me her kidneys had failed and she probably had less than thirty-six hours to live. I called Dad in Belfast who had left Barbie's side just before my arrival. He returned from Belfast to Boston just at the end of Barb's life as she rallied. We three reminisced about the animals we had cared for and loved and she remembered some I had completely forgotten. She called her girls and told them she loved them. We told her that Liz and Jackie would be fine and it gave her peace. My sister had remarkable courage and touched many lives. Her wit and exceptional story telling attracted people to her wherever we went. It was heart warming to see a true economic cross section of Americans sitting side by side at her funeral. She fit in and was accepted and loved by everyone.

Several months earlier she had asked me to take her girls if anything happened to her. I told her that I just couldn't. It was difficult for me, a single parent, to raise two children. I loved her daughters so much I felt like was nearing a breakdown and I just couldn't function well and certainly didn't feel I could give them what they needed. She understood why I could not have moved her girls in with us. Luckily my brother Bob and his partner Coral agreed to welcome Liz who was eighteen and Jackie sixteen, into their home. Liz had a career in finance and now with her husband Erik is doing a spectacular job raising four children in New Jersey and in their summer home near the camp in Hanover and Jackie is now a neurologist in Philadelphia. Brother Bob did a tremendous job, much better than I could have done. They are amazing adults and remind me of their mother in so many ways. Five years after Barb was diagnosed she died. She was thirty-nine. I didn't know if I would ever recover. Once Barbie became ill, Dad stopped drinking.

It had taken him all of those years. She gave him a purpose and he took care of her, charted her progress, and was in touch with her nearly every day. I saw him as a different man, the man my mother loved and the man I had known as a child. We had many days together sitting on my front porch or going to lunch, just talking. I cared for him again. About six months after Barbie died Dad got the flu and when he felt better he came to Bangor to my office as he often did, and explained that he would not go through something like that flu again. He had retired to Belfast which was about a forty-five minute drive from me and he didn't tell me he had been sick. He had suffered heart attacks previously and his doctor had told me he didn't have long to live. While Dad was talking to me, he had his head in his hands and his elbows on my desk, just looking at me. I knew how sick he was. I told him,

"Don't give up."

He said he wouldn't. He never would. Dad died about three weeks later on Mom's birthday. Dad for years had tried to convince me to take over his business and be the executor of his Will and I declined because I thought my brothers would "gang up on me" and I told Dad that. He thought they may, and got a friend of his to execute the Will but things became a mess and extremely hurtful to me as my brothers ganged up on me anyway. Brother Bob threatened to sue me through his lawyer to mine. My lawyer showed his lawyer that Bob didn't have cause at all. He is my brother for heaven sakes. He wanted gem stones which Dad had willed to Liz and Jackie. Much later he got them directly from them.

Dad wanted to will me the contents of his house and I told him I thought it would be better if that went to the boys. I didn't want to go through his clothes, guns, etc. On four occasions in front of two of his friends Dad said he knew Jim would give me the female things like his jewelry because Jim had told Dad several times he didn't want anything. He kept trying to convince himself that my brothers would do the right thing. Well, I ended up paying for the jewelry and anything else I wanted from Dad's house, even Saltines I had for lunch. Jim was handing things of Dad's out to a new girlfriend in front of me and was giving things away to strangers. I know he was in a daze as we all were, but I think Dad would have been very disappointed. Throughout the day Jim sold the contents to Dad's house I remained calm because I felt strongly that Dad was watching and knew what my brothers were putting me through. That helped me a lot. I had hoped to be able to keep the heirlooms that Dad wanted me to have to pass down in the family. I felt my heart was broken for my own brothers whom I loved so much distrusted me for no reason. Sure, they both later apologized and told me they had been jealous of me and it was devastating. I was close to Dad for the last five years of his life and had encouraged brother Bob to visit him after Dad had been in my office after recovering from the flu but Bob didn't visit him. The night Dad died was a strange one for me. I had called him before I left for Switzerland to see if he wanted me to bring him back anything and Dad said he didn't want anything. It was about three weeks after his visit to my office. He mentioned that he had the hedge trimmed that day. I later found out that he had trimmed it himself. Anyway, I went to dinner with friends when I arrived in Basel and I couldn't eat. I felt that something was wrong. I went back to my hotel room early, fell asleep, only to awaken at midnight with many, many questions for Dad. "Do you remember this? Where were we when such and such happened? "

My mind was filled with questions that only Dad could answer. My head was swirling and filled with places forgotten from childhood. One place would come into mind, then another and another. It was like a slide show. I did finally fall asleep and at three in the morning, Swiss time, brother Jim called to tell me that Dad had died of a massive coronary in his sleep.

I waited until six to call my friends in Basel, a very long three hours, and they drove me to Zurich where I got a return flight to New York. John gave me a sedative to take but I could not stop crying and sat in the back of the plane so I could lie down. Once landed I had to change airports in New York. I walked out of the airport with one large suitcase to a cab stand and a line of cabs out front. A cabbie with a cab hat on took my bag and I followed him as he walked across the road to the parking lot where his van was parked. I didn't see a meter and I said,

"This is not a cab."

His response? "Oh, yes it is."

He pointed to one of the two women in the cab and said, "I am taking that passenger to Queens" and the other woman agreed. He threw my suitcase in and as I stepped inside I saw an unmade bed in the very back of the vehicle. There was no way out and I have never been more frightened in my life. He drove from Kennedy airport to the LaGuardia Airport the long way, and I began to play on the sympathies of the women. The three of them were speaking Spanish and I told them that my father had died and my family was waiting for me to get home for the funeral and I had to get there as soon as possible. I knew the trip was usually about twenty minutes and it had been almost forty-five minutes by that time. We did finally arrive at LaGuardia airport and I opened my wallet and showed them that all I had was a fifty franc bill from Switzerland which I knew was worth less than twenty dollars. The fee for the trip was usually nineteen dollars and the fake cabbie had asked me for twenty-four dollars for the ride. All three were happy thinking they got fifty dollars for the trip. I had hidden my U.S. money in another part of my purse, which was probably the only thing I did right that day.

As I carried my suitcase by the cab station at the second airport, red faced from crying and the unbearable heat, the lead cabbie at the stand asked me if something was wrong. As I continued walking I told him that I had taken a cab but it wasn't a cab. He wanted to know if I got the tag number. I thought about it while I was in the cab, but once out of that vehicle I did not dare to look back. He asked if I wanted a ride up to the terminal. No way. When I got home to Bangor my friend Paul told me that there had recently been an article about Gypsy cabs in the "New York Times," and that was my experience with a Gypsy cab.

We had a quiet wake for Dad on Fathers' Day but later on had a bang up jazz jam session in his memory at the Pilots Grill Restaurant in Bangor. The facility was full and brother Jim had arranged the whole program. It started with Jim putting Dad's banjo on a chair onstage. Jim stood on stage alone and played Barb's favorite song on his bass viol, "Bye, Bye, Blackbird." Then drums and piano player were added with the musicians coming on stage from the audience and the trio did a set of well known tunes. A female jazz vocalist joined them and they brought the house down. Then a quartet followed with an added brass instrument and as each musician joined in from the audience the band became bigger and bigger. They did a Dixieland set and for a finale marched throughout the room, around the tables, playing the "Saints Go Marching In." No band ever sounded better. The people in attendance were rocking in their seats and singing along. Spirits were high. Then almost immediately the band went on to play, "Amazing Grace." We were all jolted back to reality. Tears were streaming down the faces of the musicians and the faces of just about everyone there. It was by far the most moving musical presentation I have ever seen. Dad's send off was unique and special and nine months after Barbie left us, Dad went to join her.

A week later I had a dream. Dad was walking up the driveway at his house with his sport jacket on and his pipe in his hand and I was thrilled.

"I thought you were dead," I said.

He replied, "No I'm not."

"I thought you were dead, I thought you were dead," I repeated.

"No, I am alive." I then woke up. Crying.

Howard Pond

FIFTEEN

FULFILLMENT
Making a difference.
1983-1992

My major goal was to raise two responsible, loving adults and with God's help, we did. It took three of us, Rhonda, Rob and me. I also threw myself fully into my work. I think the part most difficult for me with the move to Bangor was the complete lack of a private life. I knew many people and with Maine's largest newspaper, twelve radio stations and four television networks, I was interviewed probably every week about different issues. I lived in a glass house. I worked twelve to sixteen hour days and attended thirteen Christmas parties one year there.

I absolutely loved my job though and learned that one person could make a difference but for many years I was playing Supermom and living a stressful life that would eventually catch up with me.

My younger brother, Bob Howe.

CAREER HIGHLIGHTS

- Working with several businesses to locate to the Rockland and Bangor areas.

- A group trip to Anderson, South Carolina, to show The Chamber members there why Bangor was rated higher than Anderson in a Money Magazine Liveable Cities Survey.

- Ten trips to Switzerland including two trips for Bangor businessmen.

- Public speaking, particularly before the Basel Rotary Club in Switzerland and being interviewed by a reporter for the largest newspaper in Europe. The article was in German and I couldn't understand a word of it.

- Attending a Beer Festival in Germany and being introduced and warmly welcomed as a citizen from the USA.

- Becoming the first woman in the Bangor Rotary Club.

- Using the Russian language phonetically in a speech before Russian dignitaries.

- Being presented by the Governor, Maine's highest award for tourism achievement.

- Creating a partnership with Saint John, New Brunswick, Canada.

- Exporting Maine products to Switzerland for the first time as a result of the Bangor Basel Trade Mission.

- Organizing the Bangor Basel Trade Mission.

- Being given a trip to Hawaii as a thank you from the Marines there for the Troop Greeting.

- Bangor winning Midland, Texas, Community Achievement award.

- Being invited to New York to see the "Today Show"

- Being invited to the White House for a meeting with government officials.

- Fundraising and completing a Chamber building Renovation and addition.

- Sitting in a truck and talking to actor Karl Malden as he shared his chocolate chip cookies with me and having a corsage pinned on my gown by Ricardo Montelban. They were filming <u>Captains Courageous</u> In Rockland Harbor.

- Wow, what a job! The organizations would not have been as successful without the thousands of volunteers I had the pleasure of working with over the years. They made everything happen.

SOUTH CAROLINA

The editor of the <u>Bangor Daily News</u> called me because he had read about a fundraiser the Anderson, S.C., Chamber of Commerce was organizing called the "Beat Bangor Bash." Their city was rated lower than Bangor in a Livable City Survey in "Money Magazine," and they could not understand how Bangor could have done so well. We in Bangor got a committee together at our Chamber and sent the Anderson board members a picture with some of our board members posed at a board room table in the snow with their skis sticking out of a snow bank behind them. We also sent them a box of joke items to auction off at their fundraiser. Their promotional committee was called the Golden Goose Society so we got over one thousand ping pong balls, painted them like gold eggs, and put numbers on each one with the cities' scores in black magic marker.

About ten of us wearing black tee shirts with "Bangor Brigade" printed on the back, flew to South Carolina and at midnight arrived at the Anderson Chamber office. We covered their huge Chamber sign with one we had brought from Bangor saying Bangor Chamber of Commerce. We also put ping pong balls all around the property and covered their building with posters. Just as we finished, members of the Sheriff's Dept. arrived. They thought the whole episode was humorous and shortly afterwards the Anderson Chamber members drove into the parking lot. We had hoped to sneak out unseen but were invited in for drinks and met some very friendly people. We returned to our rooms in Greenville around two in the morning and flew back to Bangor the next day.

A few months later the Anderson group flew to Bangor where we met them on the airport tarmac with huge snow plows that brought them from their private planes to the terminal. We had also placed a mascot they sent us, a large toy pelican, on top of the Bangor Paul Bunyan statue, had bottles of water labeled "white lightening" in their rooms, and showed them around Bangor. They were impressed and surprised Bangor was such a large, metropolitan city for prior to their visit they thought Bangor was a small city in the sticks. Several of the merchants handed our guests gifts as they visited their stores and they loved the Bangor area. We had many other visitors from Anderson that summer and the two cities battling back and forth made CNN and other national news agencies. Bangor could not have paid for the free, positive publicity it received.

SWITZERLAND

The director of Bangor International Airport called me and suggested the Chamber find a way to thank Balair Airlines for refueling in Bangor as they came to the States from Europe. I called the Chamber in Basel and asked to speak to someone who could speak English. John came on the line and throughout the next few weeks we organized about sixty business people and chartered part of a Balair plane and we took the group to Basel. While there, the Bangor restaurant owners met with Basel chamber members and cooked up a typical Maine feast with lobster, corn on the cob, blueberry cake and all the fixins in one of their restaurants. Our business people were matched with their counterparts and they ate side by side and taught them how to crack lobsters as they discussed business.

The itinerary was planned by the Chamber there and included tours of the country, a fashion show, a trip up one of the Alps highest peaks by train, the Yungfrau, and five star accommodations and restaurants. It was first class all the way.

Our Chamber reciprocated the next year and hosted two business groups from Switzerland in Maine. There became some great connections between the two countries and one of Maine's largest blueberry processing facilities was exporting blueberries directly to Basel as a result of the trip. Maine lobsters were shipped to the area, a grocery store chain in Maine began carrying Swiss chocolate, fondue, and other Swiss products with its own display area, and students came to Maine to study. One student visited to work as a hotel restaurant cook. Many friendships continue today as a result of the Bangor Basel Trade Mission.

The Chamber Board was very supportive. During our first Swiss trip, two Directors arranged for me to stay an additional week in Switzerland. They bought groceries for the kids at home and hired the sitter so I could stay.

Another director brought groceries to the house when I entertained company from Switzerland. I may have been a single parent but I didn't feel a financial burden.

John and Bernadette showed me all around their country and after a few trips there I had also visited Germany, France, Italy, Austria and Liechtenstein. They are wonderful people and tour guides. In Italy, Bernadette and I went to a boutique in Milan and I bought a beautiful Royal blue winter coat. Bernadette took the price tags off thinking we would get through customs without paying tax. Well, we got stopped and she had to go inside and be interrogated for about forty five minutes. She ended up paying the fine although she wouldn't tell me what it was. I love Basel and while in the town center I was beginning to recognize and speak with business men I had met there previously. I began to understand the language, a little bit, but still carried a little piece of paper with a street listed on it when I went on the tram.

THE TODAY SHOW

The general manager at the NBC News affiliate, Margo, invited me to a dinner the night before the Fourth of July festivities to meet Willard Scott as I was to do a short remote with him the next day on the "Today Show." I settled down at the further end of the table from him and he asked me to go up to meet him which I did.

The night before, two men I had met on the Mt. Mitchell, a NOAA Ship moored in Rockland, called me at home and asked me out to dinner. They picked me up in an older model light blue Cadillac convertible with the top down and we went to a small Bangor restaurant and had a great time.

The next day I was asked to transport Willard around and he was scrunched up in my Subaru as we drove around Bangor. He said he wanted to go to my house for coffee. I said no. The dog was shedding and the house needed to be vacuumed. He offered,

"You can make the coffee while I vacuum." He was really being humorous.

"No, thanks."

My friends drove by in their Cadillac in the Fourth of July parade as Willard and I were judges on the grandstand together that day. They wore Groucho Marx glasses and noses and they kept shouting at me, "Hey, Ma," as I tried to ignore them. Willard asked me if I knew them and although I was continuing to try to keep up my professionalism I told him rather meekly yes.

He enjoyed their antics and was laughing at them. Willard then asked me to go to New York to visit the "Today Show." I declined several times.

In August I was going to Newark, Delaware, for Institute. I had made friends with a Rockland neighbor, a travel planner, who had moved back to New York to be with his family who were from Romania and lived in a neighborhood inhabited by Romanian immigrants. Tom invited me to visit and stay at his home and his mother invited the entire family in to meet me. It was like going to the old country. Tom's family had been in New York four years and his mother, a sweet, lovely hostess, spoke only Romanian. There were four huge pots on the stove with stuffed cabbage, beef and gravy, spinach and egg soup, and sauerkraut. It was wonderful. The apartment was warm and homey with a narrow, very hot and muggy kitchen, old fashioned wallpaper in the living room where I slept, and clothes lines out the kitchen window. Tom's mother cooked and picked up constantly and wouldn't let anyone help. The family was very close and the home vibrated love. What an experience for me!

That evening Tom, his sister and her fiancé and I walked to a Romanian restaurant nearby and heard Romanian and Gypsy music played by a violin duo. There was a singer in their native costume and a comedian there as well. It was strange to be with people who laughed at the jokes when I didn't understand any of them. The next day I took my first subway ride into Manhattan with them. We walked block after block looking in store windows and had drinks at an inviting bar and picked up Chinese for supper. I bought Tom's mother a window fan for the kitchen which she badly needed and she liked.

The next day, I was in a cab on the way to 30 Rockefeller Plaza at 6:15 am. I slept very little I was so afraid I wouldn't wake up in time. I entered through large doors into a lobby with gorgeous brightly lit shops on either side of the entrance way with sparkly things on display, and walked to the news stand and asked directions to the "Today Show." When I arrived at NBC studios there was a guard by a sign which read, NBC Security. I went over to him and he immediately said, "You must be Scottie." Whew, was I relieved. Anyway, he told me to take the elevator to the third floor and that someone would meet me there. When the elevator doors opened there was Willard with arms outstretched and a boisterous greeting.

We went into the studio where there were five sets and fifteen production people working.

Jane Pauley turned and said hello and she is much smaller and more attractive in person. She put on make-up during each break which I thought was a bit much.

Bryant Gumbel was impressive simply because he made comments on news items and tapes they ran. He would say so everyone could hear,

"What a yo-yo. What are we doing with him on? Let's nuke that tape next time."

He was in complete control of the show. At one point Bryant threw his coffee mug to an assistant off camera for a refill, his staff person missed catching it, and it shattered everywhere.

Larry King, one of the guests that day, came flying by like he was the most important person there. John Palmer, the news man at the time, stopped and spoke to me and made me feel comfortable.

After the show, Willard and I left and walked down the street to what I believe was the Waldolf Astoria. People would recognize him and shout his name just as we got beyond them. Willard would turn and speak to them. He was appreciative of his fans. We walked into the hotel, up some wide marble steps to the right and up to one of the fine dining restaurants inside. We both had eggs benedict which I thought were outrageously expensive at the time and we talked about our personal lives, money, jobs, power, and our experiences. It was amazing how well we clicked. He said, "For two open, down to earth people, what did you expect?" He told me he had an opening for a secretary but seeing me in New York he didn't think I would be comfortable there. I told him he was right and that I had two children I would not move from their schools. Willard made sure I got back to Tom's with his NBC driver and it was an experience I will never forget. We did speak on the phone a few times after getting together, even on that day. He is a good person.

THE WHITE HOUSE

Another unusual experience I had was a visit to the White House. I received a post card in my Bangor office in which I was invited to Washington D.C. to meet with some "high government officials." I thought it was a joke. I had a Chamber friend, Wayne, who would often pull practical jokes on me, so I set the card aside. A few days later just before throwing it out, I decided to call the phone number listed and was astonished to hear, "The White House." I was asked for some information so a security check could be done on me and was given directions to give the cab driver for entrance onto the White House grounds. I was floored it was for real. I had a couple of weeks before the event so I went out and bought a new black suit and a white blouse and made plans to fly down.

When I arrived at the White House I walked up a brick path to a circular building with guards where I checked in. Then, I walked by myself through the rose garden which had all the flowers and plants labeled, and on into the building. There was a coat check there and a group of people had started to line up. None of us knew why we were there and it seemed as if there was one representative from each state. All of us were thrilled to have been invited. To me, it was like a dream standing there. Soon we were ushered upstairs to the Green Room where thirteen television cameras were set up in a row. I recognized Sam Donaldson, a reporter.

Members of Reagan's cabinet came to the podium for a briefing on Central America. Speakers included: George Shultz, Secretary of State; Rear Admiral Robert W. Schmitt, USN Deputy Director, Defense Intelligence Agency; Elliot Abrams, Asst. Secretary of State for Inter-American Affairs; Lt. Gen. Colin Powell, National Security Advisor to the President; and President Ronald Reagan. Following the presentation we were free to ask questions and for once I kept my mouth shut.

President Reagan came out to the podium last and spoke longer than I expected he would. I do have his speech on tape as Rhonda and Rob were watching and taping the Evening News from the television at home. I did notice that the President wore excessive make-up. The function was a news conference with updates on the United States relationships in Central America.

After the time at the White House I headed back to the airport for the flight home. I only made it as far as Boston.

When we landed our plane skidded back and forth on the runway and you could see the runway lights one minute and they were under the plane the next. There was absolute silence on the plane and when the plane stopped I asked my seat mate if he realized we were in trouble and he said yes. I guess everyone did. We were the last flight to land in Boston that night because a Northeaster was coming in and all flights were cancelled. Throughout the process at the airport a group of us had been sitting together for most of the day and I discovered that one of them lived next to a Chamber director friend of mine near Logan

Airport so he drove me to my friend's house and I spent the night there. The next day I made it home.

I did travel about three times a year by plane then and felt free and loved it. There seemed like no obstacle was too much to overcome to me then. I was finding independence, fulfillment and happiness in my work and with my children.

Along with the great experiences, there are some better forgotten although they never will be. I was in Augusta to attend a conference and went into the meeting room early to help with setting up. Only one person, Jack, was in the room and the minute he saw me he told me I had two different shoes on, one black and one navy. I told him I had the matching pair in my room and rushed back upstairs to change. After another meeting where I spoke before about one hundred people in Bangor, I received a call in my office from an attorney who kindly asked,

"Are you into a new fad or something?"

When I asked her what she was talking about she told me I had on two very different earrings. I laughed but wondered how many others noticed but didn't say anything to me. After speaking to her and taking off my earrings, I walked out of my office and asked the staff to please tell me if they ever notice anything out of place with my appearance.

Sharon, the Chamber's strong, intelligent, well liked executive assistant piped up,

"You sometimes have your lipstick on crooked."

Luckily I noticed another problem before anyone else did. I was sitting at my desk about nine in the morning before I had any meetings. I happened to look down at the back of my calf and there was a dog biscuit stuck behind my panty hose. I was laughing so hard I showed the staff. Our Pomeranian, BB, had apparently hidden the biscuit in the clothes basket and I didn't even notice it when getting dressed. I was always in a hurry cramming as much as I could into every minute.

Much sooner than I wanted, I experienced the Empty Nest Syndrome. Rhonda left and found a good job in Northeast Harbor. Rob left too and worked in Boston. When they were both gone it was very difficult for me. We three were family. After three months alone I told a friend he and his friend could move into rooms in my house. It was a very good arrangement. We all had things to do with keeping up the house and with all of us working we saw each other over coffee in the morning and that was about it. It was a comfortable situation for me because it increased my income and I began to relax a little. I didn't feel the entire burden of the house was mine anymore.

One early morning I received a call from the airport director and he told me that Saddam Hussein was releasing American captives and that they may come through Bangor on their return to the States. We were ready in case we were called on by the government and had facilities and products in place for their return. We had several meetings and plans to separate airport hangers into different sections, medical, food, clothing, etc., were in progress. I had called Chamber members and they had generously donated truck loads of food, drinks, magazines, clothing, etc., which we stored in the Chamber board room. We then heard that the ex-hostages were arriving in another location but that the troops would be leaving from and returning to Bangor for Operation Desert Storm. John, a board member, and I loaded our cars and took the donated goods up to the airport for the troops. We set up a couple of long tables and kept them loaded with goodies for months.

On that first dark night, about twenty Green Berets arrived and lined up and sang, "The Green Berets." It brought tears to our eyes and their heartfelt, sincere love of country will be with me forever.

There were perhaps six of us there all night that first night shaking hands and welcoming troops home. As the community got word of the activity at the airport, arrival times were announced on the radio, and increasing numbers of citizens joined in. The airport staff arranged area bands to perform and the John Bapst band played often. Two hundred fifty soldiers from the Eighty-Second Airborne arrived on another day and a soldier picked up a saxophone from a student and sat in with the band and played solo, the "Star Spangled Banner" as tears rolled down his face. There wasn't a dry eye in the terminal and by that time there were probably one hundred plus troop greeters there. Eventually the airport had as many as one thousand troop greeters meet the incoming flights and the generosity and love of the people of Bangor spread throughout the country. The patriotic gesture continues today. The Chamber members and citizens throughout Maine and New England eventually greeted more than 60,000 troops from more than 220 flights from Desert Storm in four months. It was incredible and brought a positive message of Bangor and its people throughout the world. We received prayers, beautiful letters, and donations from around the country. One of my favorite letters was from the son of Francis Gary Powers who had been shot down over the Soviet Union while flying a U2 spy mission. I had said prayers for Powers when it happened and I was sixteen. In 1962 Powers was exchanged in a well publicized spy swap. With donations received the Chamber funded a display with awards and letters for the troops and greeters which is located in the Bangor International Airport and presented an event to thank the troop greeters and we watched Generals Charles Horner and John Yosock lead the band in patriotic songs.

SIXTEEN

JIM
My love, King Bubba
1988-forever

The fall bouquet of flowers arrived at the office and the unsigned attached card read, "I have your hat." I immediately asked my staff if they had any idea where I had left a hat. What hat? I had no idea but I was curious and called the florist. I was told that the flowers had been sent by Jim Bell. I called him and thanked him and later got the hat back. Jim had taken me to a nice seafood restaurant for dinner and shortly after that, although I had been sick with pneumonia, he offered to get me out of the house and we drove to Bar Harbor. He was very thoughtful and caring but I only knew him from what my sister Barb had said about him. Jim, Barb and I had gone to lunch one Secretaries' Day years before because he had been my sister's boss for ten years, but I only saw him occasionally when I visited her at the Air Force Recruitment office where she worked with him throughout those years.

"Jim is the nicest man I know and is like a brother to me," Barb told me. She told me that more than once. They were close enough to have played a number of practical jokes on each other. She adored him and he let her have all the time off she needed during her illness. He also submitted her name for Secretary of the Year, a national award, which she won more than once. I too thought he was a very nice man. About a month before I dated Jim, I had taken a walk in the snow and decided that I was ready to share my life, to settle down. I said a prayer that someone would come into my life and I knew Jim had been sent to me from God. It was very clear to me. It had only been a month.

Judy and Paul, my friends, had encouraged me not to dismiss Jim as I was so quick to do with others. That helped because it caused me to think and helped me see what a wonderful man Jim was and what was best for me. Jim and I had many things in common with similar values, love of children, the "oldies," and we felt very comfortable with each other as if we had been close for a long time. During the nearly eight years I was single I dated some but melded more and more into my career leaving a personal life behind. A personal life became non-existent. If I wanted a party I had one through work. I was much too busy, all of the time. Without either of us recognizing it, Jim and I were beginning to bring a personal life back to me and we enjoyed being together. While having take-out in the car one night Jim said,

"I have four words I have been wanting to ask but think it may be too early."

I knew what he was thinking even though it was only our fourth or fifth date and I asked him what he wanted to say. I was very surprised but being so much like myself I understood the urgency. May as well get it over with and not have to worry about asking again. So…

Jim asked me if I would marry him. I said I would have to think about it and several things went through my mind. Am I ready? How will the kids take it? I said yes. I knew it was right. Jim was the right man for me. I didn't want to be away from him. We were married within four months.

Jim and I always enjoyed visiting with Judy and Paul at Green Lake. One snowy day when the temperature was three below zero, we joined them for a skiing party. A group of us snowmobiled and skied into the woods where Judy and Paul had set up a snow bank lunch. There was a table, table cloth, candles, wicked good food, and a bonfire near a small wooden bridge that crossed a brook. The snow was newly fallen over perhaps three feet of old snow and our parked skis stuck out of the snow banks on either side of the trail. Wine was also propped up into the snow and all the couples were joyous and friendly. It was one of the best parties I have attended and even though Jim was frozen, he had fun, too. I appreciated the fact that he would do new things and was spontaneous.

Our four offspring took our wedding plans differently. Sean was very happy for his father. I had met him when he was younger but again met him one night when he came to our house alone and introduced himself. I was amazed at his confidence and liked him immediately. Of the four I think Sean put his parent first and was the most supportive. Sean has a big heart and is sensitive and caring. He is living with a very serious brain injury from an accident. On full disability he is unable to work and devotes all of his time to his American Bull dog, Callie. Sean has conquered more than any of us in his battle to live a comfortable life. He lives about four miles from us in Florida.

Jim and I drove to Augusta where Rob was working and told him our plans. His first words were,

" I won't be the man of the family anymore."

I didn't realize he had seen himself in that position but it nearly broke my heart. At that moment, I realized that the family threesome we had enjoyed through more than seven years, would be changed, broken. We had been close in our home in Bangor but

Rob and Rhonda were both out of the home and we were all moving on. We were beginning a new family.

Rob lives in Oregon now and is Vice President of Operations at a dot com company. He has been with the company for several years and has been very productive and successful. He travels in the United States and Europe about fifty percent of the time and has been there for Rhonda and me when we have needed him. He has a spiritual depth that is very inspiring.

Rhonda seemed confused with our plans to marry and although neither she nor Sean or Rob was living at home, she was still testing out her independence. She seemed happy for us but she was guarded. She just didn't seem too sure about the idea. She was working in the Portland area at the time.

Shay was only sixteen when Jim and I decided to marry and she lived with us afterwards. I didn't realize that Jim had just recently finalized his divorce after a two year separation and Shay was grasping onto Jim for some stability in her life. She and Sean had both rejected their mother although Jim encouraged them to keep up their relationship with her. Shay was insecure and needed love but could not accept me. She didn't want to let go of her father for many years and we had more than a few difficulties. Shay and I have agreed that the details can be read in Shay's memoirs in the future. We are now like mother and daughter and have overcome the hurdles. Recently she went on a mission to Tanzania, Africa, and has set up a foundation, 1ndoto.com which is raising money to support the children there. This year she has spent more time in Africa than here in Florida. She has found her calling and is completely dedicated to making life better for others.

Each of our four adult children has accepted Jim and me in their own way. They all appreciate having another brother and sister and decided early on that they were not stepbrother and stepsister, they were brother and sister.

Although our first years of marriage may have gone smoother had we waited to marry, it was a good decision. I loved having Jim with me to talk to about my work, to share feelings and confidences, and to enjoy little things together. It was great having him drive so I could watch the world go by as a passenger, and Jim was more than willing to help with household chores. His support was tremendous. In spite of the great situation I was in, I felt then that marriage had brought more stress to my life. Shay and I getting along badly bothered me a lot and Jim didn't seem to notice that he, Shay and Sean were still a family of three, and I was on the outside. It was horrible for me as I had felt we would all be a family. I was becoming increasingly paranoid but when I spoke to three of Jim's male friends at different times, they said they could see what was happening and felt my feelings of being left out were justified. We would talk to Jim but he just blocked it out. He had an extreme amount of stress too, particularly over Sean, but it seemed that when he didn't want to see something, he wouldn't listen to any one. He simply ignored it. He thought I was asking him to choose between me or his children. That wasn't my intention at all. When we moved to Florida both Shay and Sean moved to Florida too with Sean down the street and Shay in a house across the street from us. It wasn't until Shay moved away that she was able to pull away from her father and stand on her own. Sean is still very dependent on Jim but since his accident Jim has been his strong supporter and has assisted him in any way he can. Jim is the only family member Sean confides in, the only friend he has. That puts a tremendous amount of pressure on Jim.

Prior to leaving the Chamber I realized that I had to slow down. For many years I had lived with meetings back to back, twelve hour work days or more and was sleeping less than six hours a night. I was still doing that up to my last week at the Chamber. It caught up with me. I began having medical problems, surgeries, and began to slip into depression again. I clearly remember the night that something seemed to be happening to me. I was at a concert at the Auditorium and I was the only person to be introduced to the audience. It pleased me but when I stood up I almost fell over. I was extremely dizzy and had difficulty keeping my mind in the present. I felt sick to my stomach and couldn't understand what was wrong. Another trip to the doctor got me a heart catheterization and gall bladder surgery. Great.

Rob Rhonda Shay Sean
On our wedding day, December 8, 1988.

Within the next few months I became confused and found it difficult to read and write and felt smothered around people. As my fears increased I knew I should get help but didn't know where to turn. The counselor I knew was in Rockland and I didn't want to take the time from work and the kids it would have taken me to go there. Jim and my friend Judy didn't sense that I was in trouble. Even if they asked I would have told them I was fine. That actress again. To parallel my problems was an incoming director who seemed like two people to me. I had supported him for the position and didn't discover these things about him until it was too late. Three very good directors of Bangor organizations resigned because of him and I was his next target. Two of the people closest to him told me that they knew he was trying hard to get me out of my job. They told me they were disappointed that I didn't hang in there. Had I been my usual self, strong and self confident, I would have faced the problem in the initial stages and handled it but I just didn't have the strength to bother. I had always had very supportive Chairmen but he and another on the Board at the time were the exception.

The director, Wilbur, came into my office one morning wanting to know what another director on the Board, Mark, had said to me about him. It wasn't flattering. I didn't tell him. I always prided myself on my ethics and I refused. Early the very next morning he came back into the office. He was furious and shouted at me,

" You tell me what Mark said about me. You should not know anything that I don't know."

Can you believe that? I was floored and I was also scared to death. He shook his fist at me as his face reddened and his veins popped out in his forehead as he became increasingly angry. I gave him just enough information to satisfy him so he would leave and felt terrible that I had told him anything at all. That was not like me. Why did I give in? It truly bothered me.

He was clearly like my abusers and with help from counseling, I was able to figure it out. I just wanted to avoid conflict as I had wanted throughout my life.

I exhibited symptoms and after extensive testing at Eglin Air Force Base several years later, I was diagnosed with Post Traumatic Stress Syndrome.

At the Executive Committee meeting that week I resigned. I had a list of issues of inappropriate behavior on Wilbur's part but didn't go into it. Following that meeting Wilbur asked me to join him for a trip to a meeting at Augusta we were both attending and unfortunately I agreed. Big mistake. On the way back he yelled letting me know that he didn't appreciate me talking to board members. He had told me earlier that he wanted me to be invisible. He threatened,

" I will make sure you never work in Bangor again."

He stopped at his isolated camp and told me to wait in the car while he made a phone call. He left me there for nearly two hours and there was no way I could leave. I thought of it, believe me, but I didn't know what direction to start in. I hadn't paid any attention to how we got there. Finally a friend of ours arrived at Wilbur's camp and was shocked that I had been waiting in the car for so long because Wilbur had called him when we first arrived and he realized how long it had been. He escorted me into the camp. I had sadly resigned from a job I loved but almost laughed because I gave up. What was going on?

After leaving the Chamber I spent money given to me by Chamber members to set up an art studio and I got back to painting. Art has always been a release for me, very relaxing and satisfying. I was offered two solo art gallery shows, one in Calais and one in Orono, and painted like crazy. As usual when I get involved in something I totally immerse myself in the project whether it is cleaning a closet, planning an event, or writing this memoir. I was completely focused on the art and created twenty paintings in six months. Jim didn't like my being so disconnected from family, from everybody and from everything but I liked it and in the show in Orono, sold out two thirds of the paintings.

I spent most of the next four years in my house, sitting on my living room couch and smoking. I couldn't think straight. I couldn't remember things. If I went into a store I would get soaked from sweating. I was experiencing panic attacks. I could only walk short distances. I lost touch with people, few friends visited and I refused all invitations so when Jim said he wanted to follow his dream and move to Florida, I agreed to go. He had been working and truly had no idea how sick I was for I had been seeing my primary care physician in Bangor for medical needs throughout that time and all seemed well.

I had isolated myself and couldn't function well enough to pack my things for our move to Florida. I made horrendous business decisions and gave away items that I cherished which I am only now putting behind me. Sean and his wife at the time, Beth, helped us move and I didn't even watch the truck as it was being loaded.

Finally my friend Nancy suggested I look up agoraphobia in the dictionary after we had a discussion of what I was experiencing. I waited several months before I did that because I was afraid to learn what it meant. Agoraphobia is an irrational fear of being in open or public spaces. Great for someone in Chamber work, huh? Sometimes when I went out for a doctor's appointment I wanted to hold onto my house. I didn't want to go out. I was afraid I wouldn't get home. For two years in a row Jim and I received gift certificates for dinner in restaurants from the family. During each year I worried about having to go out to use them, but would manage to do it just before they expired. It was the only time I went out other than to a doctor or for three special luncheons with five of my favorite former Board Chairmen during the entire year.

After several years of being self-isolated, I discussed agoraphobia with Shay and she made a point to get me out. She invited me to lunch and a movie. I did not want to go but she insisted. I felt like I was in a daze at lunch and wet myself in the restroom and left my purse there before we went to the movie. Shay went back and found it. She helped me. I was experiencing panic attacks and was soaked but I accomplished Shay's mission. It didn't seem like much to me at the time but in the broader scheme of things, it was.

At Eglin Air Force Base in Florida, my newly assigned primary care physician, Dr. Belcher, began to see something was wrong as I sat in the waiting room one day crying for no reason.

After hours of testing I was diagnosed with agoraphobia, clinical depression, and post traumatic stress syndrome and was given medication and counseling and my counselor explained to me that I had suffered a breakdown. He also told me about a four star general who had a breakdown and sat in his rocking chair watching television every day. What does it mean when someone has a breakdown? No one talks about it because of the stigma still attached to any type of mental illness but it is debilitating. I thought I was dead. It felt like it. I was in another place and could not concentrate on anything. I thought if I wore my glasses people couldn't see me and the last thing I wanted to do was be with people or have people recognize me. I thought of suicide.

One day while driving the car I sat through two red lights while talking to my friend Ila and finally she spoke up and I moved on. During the worst of those months I avoided several close accidents. I had tunnel vision and just couldn't focus and should not have been driving. For nearly two years in Florida I didn't drive because I was afraid I would get lost but Jim was patient and understanding and following a talk with him I finally drove to Walmart a couple of streets away. It was difficult.

It is a strange experience when you have a breakdown. I knew I had to somehow come back to reality but it seemed just as easy to let go…totally give up and let go. It was like being in a constant day dream. I said things I didn't mean and would never have said and regret some of the things I said to this day. I had no filter and words came out of my mouth with no thought given to them. I believed that if I weren't careful, my mind would never return to normal, my brain would not take in another thing. No wonder I thought Jim was pulling away from me. I felt that everyone was against me. I got help through Eglin Air Force Base and their medical and mental health services. I used the Eglin pharmacy and my doctors were on the base and I felt I got superior care there. I was able to take classes there including one on how to handle chronic pain. I was still battling the back problems I had in college. I had felt completely lost for about six years but most of all I felt dead. Completely dead.

Two years later I began to feel better but it has been a long way back. My calendar was full daily for twenty years and now I still prefer it to be empty. I am doing better with crowds now and leave if I begin to feel uncomfortable or closed in. I know what panic attacks are and have had many over the years but they seem to be lessoning. We have lived in Florida fifteen years and I have felt pretty much like my normal self, except for forgetfulness for the last couple of years. but I've been told that some of that comes from getting older. Wow, does it ever! Of course I can always blame it on the meds.

I have reached a point now where I feel fulfilled, satisfied, and happy. Jim has been the guiding light in my life and his strength and energy have helped me. Our Florida move was a good one, especially since we have spent time at camp in Maine during summers.

We appreciate Rob's willingness to let us use the camp which he owns now. We have most of the family together at camp and it is just fantastic.

Geoff, Brother Jim, Mike

My brother Jim lived in Hanover so summer was a time for us to get together, too. His daughter Cheryl and sons, Mike and Geoff Howe live in Maine and we see them when we return there. Sadly brother Jim passed away from a coronary heart attack when he was sixty-five which was the same age Dad was when he died. Jim was playing "Time in a Bottle," one of Barbie's favorite songs that was played at her funeral, on the piano at his school when he had the attack.

Jim's musician friends gave him a dynamic tribute with musicians from throughout the country performing at the chapel at Phillips Exeter Academy where Jim taught and also at the Press Room in Portsmouth, New Hampshire, where his band played. Jim was highly respected for what he had given to his students and to jazz and his memorial services were just incredible. They were filled with emotion and tremendous jazz. Florida is an extreme change from Maine and Jim and I have felt like we have been on a tropical vacation since we moved here. The white powdery beaches and emerald waters of the Panhandle of Florida on the Gulf, are some of the most beautiful in the world. We chose an area with undeveloped forests, the "Reservation," and houses side by side so our neighbors can watch our home when we spend summers in Maine.

We do have good neighbors and I finally began getting out by volunteering at Caring and Sharing where I interviewed the homeless men, women and children in our area. I liked the work but left after three years because my medical issues made it difficult for me to be dependable. Since I always like to have a project going for a reason to get up in the morning, I began making jewelry and continued with my art.

A blessing in our lives has been two wonderful children and a loving mother and father who have been kind enough to share them with us. We don't have grandchildren and when we moved to Florida I missed having children to love. Shay was dating a man with a child and we babysat for Hugh's daughter Taylor, and watched her grow up from the age of two. She is sixteen now and has a beautiful spirit. She is a dancer, and a very special, bright and talented girl. Her young sister is three and has been a joy and we babysat her here at the house until physically I could no longer do it.

Tabitha is a "diva," an actress, a singer and dancer and warms the hearts of everyone. They both seemed to bring life back to me. I thank God for giving us their mother Amy who has so generously included us in their lives. No one could ever understand how much they have meant to me and helped me over the years.

Having retired as a Senior Master Sergeant from the Air Force after twenty-six years, Jim worked for Old Town Canoe Company in Maine almost ten years and at a car dealership in Florida for about the same amount of time. When our four adult children were successful on their own, he and I focused on each other again. We love to travel and have spent time on home improvements. He has built a brick garden walkway and a side porch, and I have enjoyed redecorating our house which is just right for us. We have been evacuated twice because of hurricanes and were hit once with several thousands of dollars in damages to our home by Hurricane Ivan.

I have never known a kinder man than Jim. He gets pleasure in making others happy and does everything he can to accomplish that, whether it is making and serving coffee or helping by carrying our ladder to another person's home. He shares or gives away almost everything he owns, chooses to have people around him rather than be alone, and understands the need for people to be themselves. He is rarely critical and gives advice when asked. He understands me and provides me with what I need to be a good wife and mother. He cares and when my neurosurgeon explained that my discs were sliding vertically instead of staying horizontally and that I am losing spinal strength and would need a wheelchair, he went right out and got me a scooter

We were both saddened when we were told by my doctor who has given me three back surgeries, that he can do no more. Although the neurosurgeon said the diving and swimming accidents may have played a part in my spinal problems he thought it was a birth defect. So we take it one day at a time and every day is a special day for us. We have always said that our marriage is 50/50 and truly it is. God knew what he was doing when he put us together.

Jim is my King Bubba and he gives me a good laugh at least once a day and after twenty four years I still love being with him. Starting with so much in common has helped us grow closer together. He goes golfing three times a week which keeps him in touch with others and keeps him fit, but most of all, keeps him happy. I am happy.

I look forward to tomorrow.

I hear laughter.

I am at peace.

I am free.

Jim relaxing in the Smoky Mountains.

Shay and Rhonda at Navarre Beach, Florida.

SCOT FREE

Rob

Sean

ELIZABETH BELL

King Bubba Jim

Shay in Tanzania, Africa

The camp on Howard Pond.

Made in the USA
Lexington, KY
02 December 2013